PSYCHOGRAPHOLOGY

PSYCHOGRAPHOLOGY

DR. DARIUSZ TARCZYNSKI

INSTYTUT NIEINWAZYJNEJ
ANALIZY OSOBOWOŚCI

(Institute of Non-invasive Personal Analysis)

AuthorHouse™ UK Ltd.
1663 Liberty Drive
Bloomington, IN 47403 USA
www.authorhouse.co.uk
Phone: 0800.197.4150

Published by AuthorHouse   01/16/2014

ISBN: 978-1-4918-8967-1 (sc)
ISBN: 978-1-4918-8965-7 (hc)
ISBN: 978-1-4918-8968-8 (e)

Cover design: Mariusz Maciejewski
Typesetting: Mariusz Maciejewski
Illustrations and reproductions: Dariusz Tarczyński
Graphological analysis: Katarzyna Tarczyńska

English translation: Joanna Bargiełowska, Mark Shepherd
Reproduction of illustrations for this version: Mark Shepherd
Originally published in Polish

INSTYTUT NIEINWAZYJNEJ
ANALIZY OSOBOWOŚCI
Plac Wolności 2
90-415 Łódź
tel.+48 42-633 56 15
biuro@nao.com.pl
www.nao.com.pl; www.inao.pl

Contents

Foreword to the Sixth Edition...ix

Introduction...xi

Prologue - A Meeting... xiii

Chapter I   Psychospace 1

Chapter II   Dynamism In Writing...................................... 8

Chapter III   Trichotomy...16

Chapter IV   Handwriting Size... 24

Chapter V   Handwriting Pressure 34

Chapter VI   The Meaning Of Margins............................. 39

Chapter VII   The Meaning Of Lines.................................. 49

Chapter VIII   Letter Connection 55

Chapter IX   The Significance Of The Letter................... 63

Chapter X   The Significance Of The Signature 71

Chapter XI   The Meaning Of The Dot On The 'i'........... 85

Chapter XII   Graphological Therapy? 92

Epilogue... 95

List of Illustrations.. 111

DARIUSZ TARCZYŃSKI

The psychologist, founder and director of the Institute Noninvasive Analysis of Personality.

He is the creator of the original methods of analysis of personality based on the interpretation of the appearance and expression.

Author of books: "How to read human in appearance", "Understanding human in appearance", "psychografology", "Key words", and press releases devoted to non-invasive analysis of personality based on the analysis of appearance, writing, or interpretation of the expression.

Guest of numerous press interviews and television programs moving non-invasive analysis of the subject's personality. Repeatedly invited as an expert on body language, communication and self-presentation for the morning programs TVP 1, TVP II

Trainer / coach with a rich, decades of experience in conducting trainings and workshops for managers and executives of companies, businesses, offices, raising manager competencies include in the field: managing and directing a team of non-monetary forms of motivation, creating the image and public speaking, negotiation techniques and influence, to cope with the emergency situation.

Adviser in creating the image of politicians, entrepreneurs, has consistently advised in the preparation of media image and statements to the media candidates for mayors.

Provides advice on the selection of staff, HR departments to provide support during interviews by training in the field of personality analysis based on handwriting research, interpretation of dress, speech interpretation.

Foreword

TO THE SIXTH EDITION

"When I wrote this book I believed that it should be addressed mainly to the younger generation."—this is how I began the foreword to the previous edition. Today I know that the transfer of the secrets of graphological knowledge in the form of a story spun from the threads of dialogue between Professor and Student attracts the interest both of young and mature readers. I leave it unchanged

wishing you a pleasant read.
The Author.

INTRODUCTION

At nineteen years of age, I became interested in psychographology. In those days, the late seventies, access to literature was limited. No self-respecting psychologist in Poland at that time officially considered graphological analysis a valuable source of information about a person's character. The fact that this technique celebrated triumphs in Germany and France—the so-called "West"—was of little importance in our socialist homeland.

When my difficulties grew in understanding this technique, when I knew that a particular handwriting feature means something and I could not understand why, I dreamed to myself that somewhere in my country is an old and good professor, a man who would teach me to understand the speech of handwriting. Problems with learning graphology turned out well for me.

The modest information that I was able to acquire from time to time, urged me on to great effort leading to an understanding of graphology and determination of the characteristics of handwriting arising from one's own thoughts.

The changes which occurred in our country also meant that literature began to appear on graphology, including literature in foreign languages. I was very proud of myself whenever I found out that my own thoughts were correct. Often, descriptions of some of the handwriting features that I found in the literature were less accurate and poorer than those in the analysis that I developed myself.

Fifteen years have passed since I became interested in graphology. There may be young people somewhere wishing to meet on their way an "old professor". I wrote this book for them, and I hope it will be useful at the beginning of the road on the adventure called graphology.

Dariusz Tarczyński

PROLOGUE

A MEETING

He was an ordinary, inconspicuous-seeming old man. He had a grey hat on his grey-sprinkled head. A grey, unbuttoned overcoat, and visible under it a dark suit of an outdated cut, he emerged from it as a neat yet slightly old-fashioned man. My attention was drawn to him because, unlike the other people on the street, he went along at a quiet, unhurried pace. It's a little strange when one sees in the hours of peak traffic a man who never hurries, but simply walks, looking around carefully. Exactly as if he was a tourist who likes to go for a walk on a cloudy Spring day, because even though the calendar said Spring, nature was insisting on proving to us that it was really Autumn. I sat on a bench across the street. I sat there often when I had a moment and watched people with great interest. I tried to guess where they were going and what they did. Yes, this man was definitely different. Suddenly he stopped and leaned against a street lamp.

It seemed that he was having trouble keeping on his feet.

Without stopping to think, I got up from the bench and ran across the road.

"Excuse me" I asked, putting my hand on his arm at the same time, "Can I help you at all?"

"I think my heart is trying to tell me something again." lifting his head he spoke in a hoarse voice, gasping for breath "In my coat pocket are some tablets, give them to me!"

After he took his medication I helped him to the other side of the street and sat him on 'my' bench. He said that he didn't want to call the doctor, that he was going there presently, he should just rest for a moment.

In this perhaps rather unusual way, I met the man who suddenly changed my life. By the time I was able to accompany him to his apartment, he had enquired of me my age, my name and what I did for a living. And, all of this he accomplished, despite his discomfort, as if it were just a passing thing.

Somehow it just came out, he wasn't being nosy. At his place, while preparing the tea and afterwards when we were sitting in chairs facing each other, drinking it in small sips, I could observe him more closely.

He was around sixty, short and slightly built. He looked at me penetratingly. Fixed lines at the corners of his eyes seemed to indicate that this old man laughed often.

"Are you a collector?" I asked.

"What makes you think that, my boy?"

I was annoyed by this expression. I would have preferred him to have addressed me a little less familiarly. I would have been much more satisfied with 'Mr Mark'.[1]

"I hope you don't mind that I addressed you that way, but with such a large age difference between us, I feel as if I were talking to my son, or even grandson. Even more so since you are talking with an old teacher who treats all his students this way, perhaps due to the lack of real sons"

"No, of course it doesn't bother me, it's even rather nice" I replied, blushing, I'm not sure why. It was just his way—surely he wasn't reading my thoughts? "I see on your desktop a strange microscope with double eyepieces, perhaps for looking at stamps or coins, and next to it I see a large magnifying glass. A biologist would probably have a somewhat different microscope?

"Excellent!" he replied, and his eyes lit up as if he had never been sick. "You're right on target—I collect people's personalities."

"How so?" I felt a shiver run down my spine at the thought that there might be something more than just heart sickness.

"You see, young man, I'm a psychographologist. A man who analyses handwritten texts and on the basis of their appearance draws conclusions about the character of the manuscript's author.

"How is this possible? Really? It is true that I have heard of such a thing, but I've never met a man whose work this was."

"This is not a very popular area of knowledge."

"Is it hard to learn?"

"Not if you are fairly observant, have intuition and a little perseverance."

---

[1] In Poland, adult strangers generally address each other as Pan/Pani (Sir/Madam) until they have agreed to use a less formal address. 'Mr Mark' (Panie Marku) would have been a way of expressing personal warmth without breaking the rules of formality.

"I'm sorry, probably everyone asks you this, but can you tell me something about me based on my handwriting? Of course, if it's not too much trouble" I added hastily. "Nothing interests us as much as ourselves, and what others think of us."

At the least I wanted to learn something, and at the same time check the effectiveness of 'divination by letters'. I assumed at the same time that the preliminary analysis would be based on generalities and elements of character which can be assigned to everyone, and where all can learn something in accordance to their qualities, find out something.

I wrote a few lines of text and put my signature under them, but as I gave him the card I was apprehensive. I do not know what I was afraid of; perhaps most people in a similar situation would feel insecure.

"You see, Mark" he said, looking at the script, "I'll just tell you a few words, since as you see, today I'm not in the best shape, and a correct analysis is a few hours' work."

At this point two thoughts fought within me. One chided me for asking a sick man for an analysis rather than leaving him as soon as possible to get some rest. The second chided him for not immediately telling me what was important, just the explanation. It was just as well that I didn't have to wonder very long.

I admit that my mouth went dry as he spoke, glancing occasionally at the manuscript. Slowly, this nondescript and seemingly innocuous old man, in the course of speaking the sentences transformed into a powerful, omniscient wizard. No, it was not a random set of characteristics. He did not and could not know that my parents were divorced, that I dream about flying or that I write poems. As for the character traits, from his mouth they sounded like praise.

"I'm not all that bad" I thought, then after a moment . . . "How does *he* know?" I was shocked.

"Master[2], please, teach me this art!" I blurted out, when he put down that piece of paper with the imprint of my soul.

"Well," he replied, smiling "One day you might be a good graphologist. Come next week at this time and I will teach you. Now, excuse me" he said, getting up from his chair "I have to rest."

---

[2] As a mark of respect, senior academics, artists and teachers are often addressed as 'Master', in Polish *Mistrzu* [pron. *meest-shoo*]. Since this reads rather strangely in English, all other instances of it are translated as 'Professor'.

I don't remember the journey home, except that it was lashing with rain. Indeed, this year's Spring has been rather more like Autumn. I couldn't sleep, twisting and turning, still recalling my encounter with this powerful man with a quiet, hoarse voice.

—Just a week . . .
. . . Will I survive that long?
. . . Just seven days.

CHAPTER I

PSYCHOSPACE

I'm very impatient and didn't want to wait for the descent of the clattering obsolete lift. I reached the second floor of the building in a few moments. My heart was beating, not only from climbing the stairs quickly. I knocked. He opened the door.

"Come in, my boy" he simply said. He walked off alone down the long corridor to the room. I closed the door and followed him, feeling the tension mount, as if he were about to become something amazing. At the same time I was afraid that my teacher, however, would withdraw his promise.

We sat on the same leather armchairs as last time, but first he suggested that I draw closer the chair in which I was to sit during our conversation, since it would be easier to show me his drawings and handwriting samples.

"If you want to learn Psychographology, we'll begin with discussions and analyses of some drawings."

"I have bought a magnifying glass" I boasted, pulling it out of a bag. I was relieved actually because up until that moment I was not sure if I could actually learn graphology. I knew from then on there would be lessons.

"That's excellent, but for today, Mark, it will be quite unnecessary."

"So, will we not be examining what is meant by individual letters, depending on how they are written?"

"You are very impatient, and graphology requires a great deal of patience. To return to your question, the interpretation of individual letters is only a supplement to the character portrait, and not the main material for inference and everything that you will learn in the course of our further activities. We'll start by getting to know the characteristics that determine our views."

"I don't understand."

"In order to fully understand, we have developed a common language. In mathematics, there are clearly defined concepts such as multiplication or division, infinity, functions, etc. In physics, it's clear what a vector is, and in

1

biology we understand what is the concept of the cell wall. In graphology, we should begin by establishing a specific language of graphological symbols. Defining some useful terms that will help us to see the world in the same way, it's still not graphology but it will greatly facilitate our study of graphology."

"So, it's a sort of language training?"

"You could say that."

I was surprised that I had to learn graphology beginning by learning what graphology isn't!

"I don't know, my boy, if you have ever turned your attention to the fact that certain gestures, attitudes and value systems are shared by many people. It turns out that there is a certain coherence, hidden deep within our information system. We don't perceive it, but we use it every day without being aware of it. People in great bursts of joy jump up and laugh, and when then feel very depressed they slouch under the influence of grief and worry."

"Maybe so" I said, "but it's probably still not a system." I was a little irritated by the banal comments that had nothing to do with graphology. He noticed it and probably smiled a little to himself.

"If you look closer at European culture, because we will speak mainly of this, you will see that the peoples of this culture, regardless of the language they use, have a common image of space—more correctly, it would be called intersubjective psychospace. Somewhere in ancient times were formed the basic directions of space, so strongly intertwined with mental and physical impressions that we are often unable to discern something differently and communicate our experiences using spatial symbolism.

"Excuse me, may I ask you for some sort of example? I'm not sure I understand." He completely surprised me with his intersubjective psychospace, for a moment I felt like I was at a scientific conference.

"It will be better if I tell you right away about all the basic directions of psychospace. I'll outline them for you directly."

In the notebook which he had in his lap, he drew a picture for a moment. He tore the page from the notebook and, continuing to speak, handed it to me.

"Study the drawing well, and I will do my best to explain to you its meaning.

The top:

In our culture this means something better. God must always be at the top, like the authorities. We call better schools 'higher'.

Someone with his nose in the air is considering himself 'above' others. One may have 'too high aspirations' or 'high morals', and even 'high-flown thoughts'—also one may say 'those on top' when thinking of people in authority.

It is also worth mentioning that climbing, conquering peaks, adding value and reaching heights, are all associated with effort. Moving from a lower to a higher degree is intimately linked with difficulty.

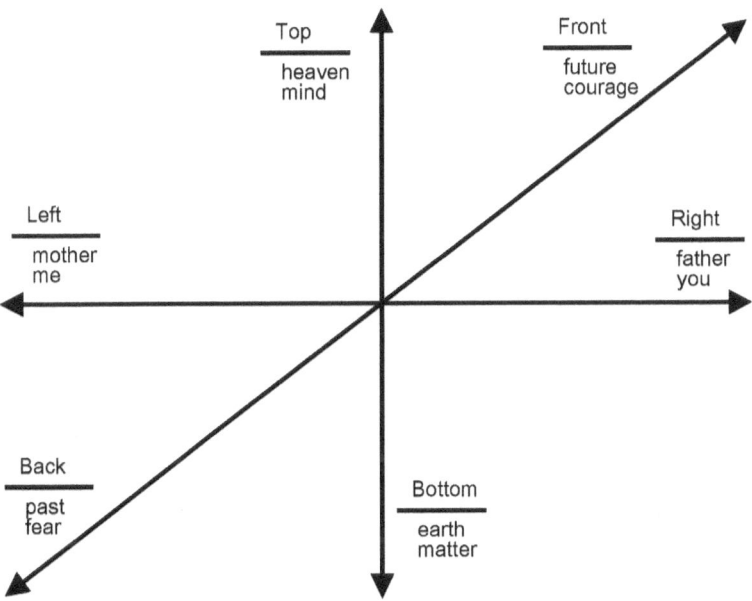

Fig. 1. Symbolic picture of the intersubjective division of psychospace.

The bottom:

This is the social lowlands; bad; worse; base instinct. Very often we feel 'low' or we speak of someone 'putting himself down'. It happens that we are driven by 'low motives'. Of course I'm giving only a few terms, in order to clarify to you the way we use directions to symbolically indicate opinions and feelings.

In our culture, better, more excellent, more valuable are always placed at the top.

"I think I'm starting to get what we are talking about, I would never have supposed that it was so crucial. It's so obvious that you just can't see it."

"Did you never consider that, for instance, shorter men are usually more go-getting; they act more boldly and dynamically; they often achieve higher social and material positions?"

"Sure! Our politicians are not particularly tall, regardless of which party they belong to. Although it happens that there are some tall ones."

"Indeed, tall men in politics and other prestigious positions are exceptions. Why? There's a simple answer. You simply need to imagine how short people feel. As you see, I don't belong to the tall group, and can say that somewhere inside myself I always feel worse in the company of taller people. Not because I am actually worse, but the feeling of inferiority stems from the lack of a few centimetres. Subconsciously I suppose I'm always afraid that others will not take me seriously enough. This lack of a few centimetres of height is a sufficiently concrete incentive towards wanting to prove my worth to other people.

If you recall, the eponymous—and short—hero in Henry Sienkiewicz's novel 'Pan Wołodyjowski', reminisces that his father instilled into him the words 'if they're not afraid of you, they will laugh at you'. Incidentally, it's strange that this intersubjective view of space is so consistent with sense of space in nature. Often before fighting, animals at all costs want to display themselves at their most imposing, puffing up fur or feathers and even rearing up on their hind legs, in order to gain height. A short man feels bad on the bus when surrounded by others taller than him. He prefers to buy a car to avoid this situation, usually the biggest car he can. Among people, physical height is replaced by social and economical status, but as you can see, not completely.

Do these terms that I mentioned also fit your perceptions related to these directions?"

"Indeed, none of these symbols run counter to my views, but what about the other directions?"

"Left side:
In our culture and symbolic viewpoint it is associated with home, beginning, birth and femininity. Writing in our culture starts from the left, which is the beginning of recording of thoughts. The left side is the symbolic centre of feelings, interior life and something weaker. There we have the heart. It's also the place of something we wish to hide, of which we are ashamed, something which is not quite 'right'. After all, untaxed work done 'on the side' is known as *lewizna*[3]. The fight for women's equality demands equality for someone

---

[3]   Practically untranslatable, this is a colloquialism similar in general meaning to the expression 'moonlighting', with its derivation from *lewo* which is left, in Polish. Effectively it is 'left-work'.

who feels they are treated worse. It's very important that you understand this well. It is that a woman is symbolically placed on the left and is someone inferior; it's not objective worth and has nothing to do with truth, but is an intersubjective term of our culture. The word intersubjective I understand as referring to people's subjective feelings which happen to be similar to the personal feelings of other people on the same subject. I'm even tempted to formulate that in this situation we are dealing with feelings that are common throughout European culture. A woman is not inferior to a man, but she feels inferior. Our culture is dominated by men. A woman normally takes her surname from her father or her husband.

Married couples prefer that the first child in their relationship is a boy. Even God in many European languages is of the male gender and we call Him Father.

This that we are talking about is not objective truth. Being higher, we feel that we are better off. The top is better. This stems from our earlier concept, however a scientist would laugh at this statement. Nevertheless the same scientist would surely feel worse if, at a meeting, symposium or a conference, he were sat on a lower chair than his professional colleagues. The left side is the site of our intuition, as it also is for our egocentrism.

Right side:
This is the direction of study of the same name "rights" [law], and also symbolic rightness [rectitude] and structure, but not necessarily justice. The right side is also connected symbolically with man, with something stronger, with logic and action. A more important guest is the one who sits on our right side. In our language is a series of moral references associated with spatial directions. The 'right' man is the one who sits or acts on the right side, that is to say in accordance with the law[4]. We think of the right side as better than the left, in a similar way that 'higher' is better than 'lower'.

Front:
Symbolically it is identified with the future. 'Go ahead/forward' means act dynamically, decisively, surely and boldly. In the diagram, the front is graphically placed above and to the right. There is within it something grandiloquent and improved, and simultaneously it is a reinforcement of

---

[4]   In Polish, the word 'prawo' means both 'law', and 'right' in the sense of 'the right to free speech'. For example, a driving licence is a *prawo jazdy*—a 'right to drive'.

right action. The front is the symbolic face, façade, life with head held high [lit. with face forward], bold. Someone can be a frontrunner, or harbinger of new ideas, forward-looking.

Back:
This is mainly symbolic fear, because we simply don't have eyes in the back of our heads, and even if we turn round very quickly, the real 'back' is blind. 'Back up', 'withdraw', these almost synonymous terms are associated with this direction. Additionally, as with the analysis of the front, the rear takes the characteristics of its neighbours from the drawing. The back/rear is a mixture of something worse, like the bottom-left side, like escaping to one's own inner world and withdrawing into the past."

"This is fantastic, so very simple as to be beyond belief."—I was impressed by this bright idea. "Why haven't I noticed this before?"

"I'm glad that you like it, Mark. Would you mind if we went for a walk? The doctor advised me to get out a little, and you Mark, after our meeting of today, will have a different outlook on the world."

We strolled unhurriedly for a while in silence. The street seemed to me to be unchanged. It was a warm, sunny day—Spring. In the city Spring can be recognized when, suddenly, as if ordered, women shed their warm clothes and walk in colourful, light dresses. I knew that it was truly Spring: the street was colourful and more joyous from swinging skirts.

"Mark" he broke the silence, "I think you already understand why the most expensive apartments and offices in the city are on the highest floors of the skyscrapers."

"Surely that's because from a height there's a wider view and the occupants of these kinds of apartments are aware that no-one else is above them."

"Excellent, but how can you explain the fact, that a hundred years ago in rented tenements the more exclusive and expensive apartments were on the first floor and the cheapest on the top floors?" I admitted that again I didn't know.

"For a very prosaic reason, Mark, which was the lack of lifts. For people from a higher class, climbing to higher storeys was exhausting and not very elegant. This example helps us to understand the fact that it's not always a single factor that determines overall, because it often transpires that another factor in the situation changes the point of view.

And perhaps you have wondered why some women like to wear hats, or . . ."

I returned home very late in the evening, went swiftly to bed, in order to ponder the whole afternoon. I felt a little embarrassed about my ignorance and inability to see such obvious facts, which the professor pointed out to me.

I was genuinely impressed by my teacher's insights and the logic with which he connected such straightforward things into a whole, having important significance for our perception.

CHAPTER II

DYNAMISM IN WRITING

During the next meeting the professor looked a little different. He was wearing light-beige striped trousers, and instead of a jacket a grey sweater. We got straight down to work. He started the lecture with no introduction.

"It's no coincidence" he said "that one of the most essential features of graphology, based on the analysis of direction, is the **slope of the writing**.

It's interpreted as reflecting the dynamism and need for contact with other people as well as the haste of the writer."

"It would never have occurred to me, but indeed, my friend Robert has handwriting that slopes very strongly to the right, and he's one of those very impatient people. He's hasty, often he does something before thinking."

"It is assumed that an angle of more than 90 degrees usually indicates an introvert, and less is typical of extrovert behaviour. You should also remember the fact that increasing the angle of slope of the letter to the left and smaller letters signifies a strengthening of the introvert features. A decreasing angle to the right and bigger letters intensifies extroversion, because leaning to the right means going forward, as we spoke about previously.

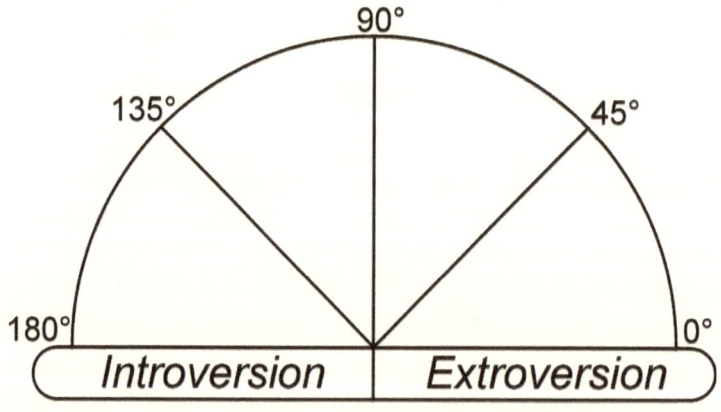

Fig. 2. The correlation between handwriting slope and dynamism in activity.

Left-sloping handwriting:

If we are not very cautious people and don't look ahead, in picking a rose hastily from the bush we can be hurt by the thorns. Then after touching the stems we snatch back our hand. In this way we learn that we have to be very careful and even to pluck flowers with care . . .

People with left-sloping handwriting are more cautious and they control their emotions. Often, in contact with others they are quite reserved and give the impression that their noses are a little in the air. People writing in this way are defined as more balanced. They follow their mind more often than their emotions. They are often good organisers, they are patient and experience consciously. They are among those who, once having hurt themselves, will not make the same mistake again. However, strenuous attention directed to their own internal worlds in continuous analysis of their own behaviours, in order to avoid their next mistakes, causes a decreasing interest in the external world. People whose left slope is very strong usually feature egocentrism.

Most often they see their environment as their opponent and take a defensive posture toward it.

Straight handwriting (perpendicular):

People with power brace their posture haughtily, proudly raising their heads. They try to proceed in a dignified manner, without vehement expostulation. If one sits higher, one has a broader horizon, one sees further. Handwriting at a 90 degree angle is the most straightforward handwriting. People writing in this way try to see more and indicate the directions which should be followed. More often, this straightness is found in the handwriting of women. Perpendicular hand-writers are defined as reasonable, good organizers, less spontaneous in action and are incapable of acting impulsively. In contact with others they are guided by moderation and logic. A perpendicular hand-writer tries to maintain a distance from the company and remain independent.

Right-sloping handwriting:

Mark, have you ever seen a runner just before the start, when crouching and fully focussed in the starting-blocks, preparing himself for running? If he crouches too much, he can fall right at the start.

In turn, in the case of too weak a crouch, a runner during the start will not be that dynamic and for sure will lose the race. In handwriting, we analyse the slope of the letters similarly; handwriting too-strongly sloped to the right can signify over-hasty action. People whose handwriting slopes to the right are extroverts, who adore action. They possess great exuberance, they easily lose control, acting emotionally.

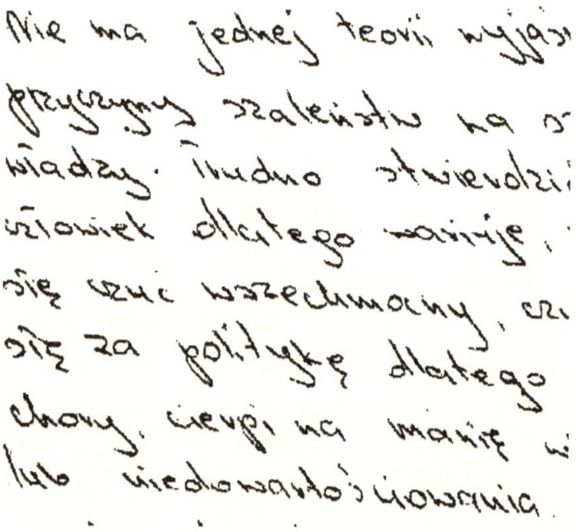

Fig. 3. Inclination of letters to the left

They approach life with enthusiasm. They want freedom and independence, and are easily influenced by other people. They are curious about the external world.

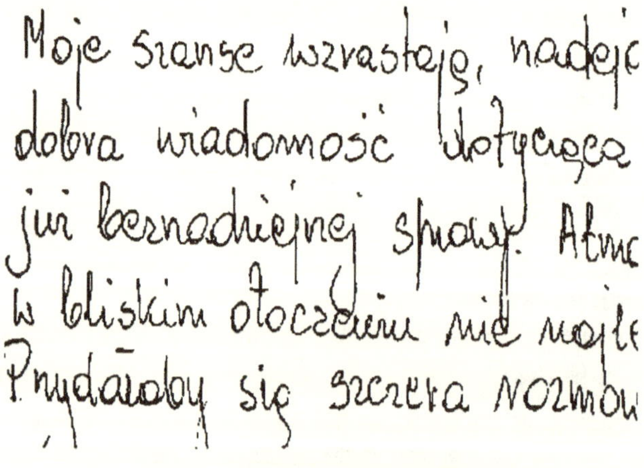

Fig. 4. Perpendicular handwriting

Their actions are largely determined by their feelings. Indeed, as previously noted, people whose letters lean to the right, often act quite involuntarily in a burst, and only then wonder about the consequences of their actions.

"Variable-slope handwriting:
A reed bends according to the strength of the wind. It doesn't resist, but easily, without resistance it bends and submits to the variable and capricious gusts. A person the slope of whose handwriting is variable, in a similar way submits to external gusts of emotions. The best illustration is that the variable slope of the letters in the script is like an encephalographic record of variation of mood. People who write in this way are unstable, full of fears and contradictions. They can be suspected of neurosis. At the beginning you may have difficulty in specifying which handwriting qualifies as variable. To facilitate the analysis you should measure the angles with a protractor. A difference of more than five degrees is regarded as having a significant value in graphology. I would not trust in someone whose handwriting slopes in different directions, since such a person can very easily

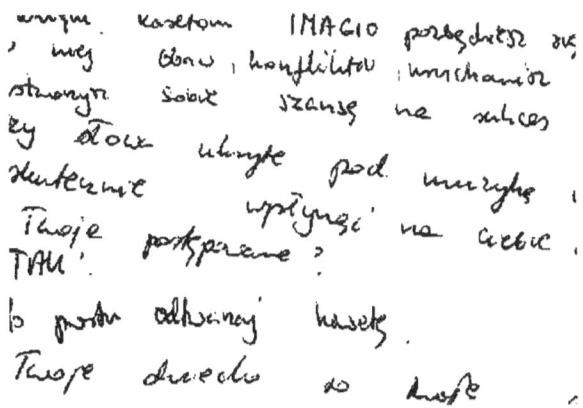

Fig. 5 Variable-slope handwriting:

change his mind according to mood. Note, however, that in the case of artists, mood swings and emotional surges are a natural expression of their creative nature. You should draw the conclusion that there are no specifically positive features, nor decidedly negative. Let's take aggression for example—for the majority of us it will create pejorative feelings. However, a man possessing this feature may use it e.g. for practising martial sports or recreate it in active, aggressive, usually more effective competition in the business arena.

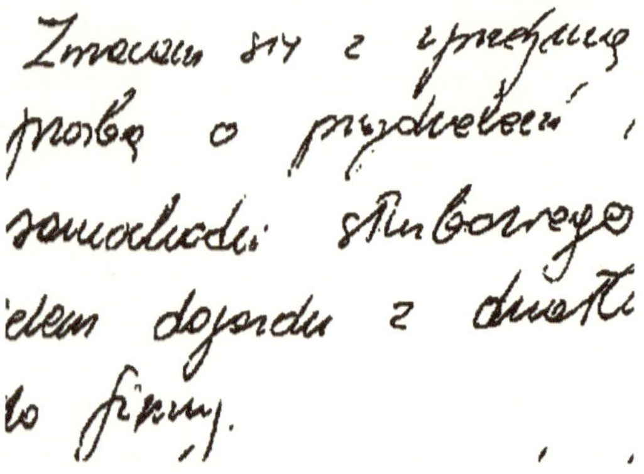

Fig. 6. Right-sloping handwriting

This figure (fig.7) should make it much easier for you to understand how to measure the angle of slope of the letter.

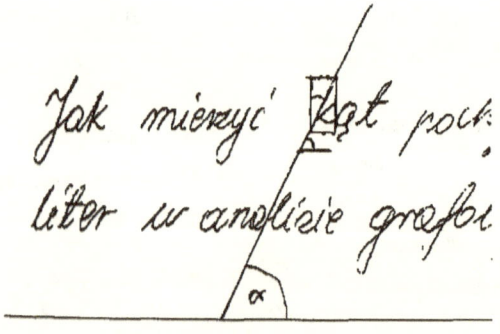

Fig. 7 Method of measuring the angle of the letters

The easiest way is to draw a straight line alongside the letter. Then, a straight line which lengthens the line of the letter two or three times, that is with all upper case letters and letters such as:

l, b, k, j, g, f etc.

I think you see more and more clearly that it is useful to know the key, even if it's only the basic symbols of the language of our subconscious, to read the content written in characters.

In psychographological analysis of relationships, the slope of the handwriting is a very important element in comparison. It is assumed that usually married couples or business partners should complement each other with regard to certain traits of character, and be like the other, to understand each other well and rely on one another. It's very difficult to make a shared business if e.g. the handwriting of both business partners slopes to the left. It's a very similar analysis in the relationships in marriage.

I know a married couple that write in exactly this way, and they can be taken as a model of the relationship between partners both having left-sloping handwriting."

"Do they behave in an unusual way?"

"Rather yes, since they have been married for several years, childless, where in one room, the wife is meditating by herself for hours each day, while the husband is praying for several hours in another room. Generally, their sole subject of disagreement is about who talks more on the telephone and who should pay the bill."

"It's ridiculous."

"For them it's certainly unpleasant—there can also be problems for couples both of whose handwritings slope to the write. When a man and woman with right-sloping handwriting meet, they are full of enthusiasm and delight. Usually they fall in love fiercely and passionately, but they will also argue with similar passion, expression and strength—even about trifles. In their case we will have the situation in which small, insignificant events can develop into serious conflicts. A young man in love, seeing his beautiful, radiant-with-joy girlfriend in a restaurant with a grey-haired older man might, for example, dash at him and punch him in anger. The girlfriend, on the other hand, being angry at her boyfriend will pour a bowl of hot soup on him, in retaliation for the embarrassment he caused her, shouting 'It's my father, moron!'.

It is generally accepted in graphology that the most suitable relationships are those where one person's handwriting is perpendicular and the other is right-sloping."

"Why, Professor?"

"I'll try to explain it with an example. Let's imagine the story of a married couple in which the woman has perpendicular handwriting and the man has right-sloping handwriting. This couple organizes a party in their house and as usual the husband will boast about his achievements, entertaining the guests by emphasizing his private and professional successes. His wife, meanwhile, will be regularly supplying food from the kitchen behaving modestly and rather quietly. The guests will believe that in that house, the husband is the boss, and moreover he himself will also be convinced of his own authority concerning important family matters.

When the guests return to their own homes, the wife will calmly and delicately point out all the gaffes made by her husband, boast about the adoration she received from one particular guest, then carefully give him a new task to accomplish. The woman in this relationship does not require explicit recognition of her authority—the husband thinks that he is the head of the household, while awaiting his next orders, since long-term planning is not his strongest suit. A partnership in which the people have identically-sloping handwriting is rather unfavourable, since it depends on the mood of the moment which of them will try to take the reins in the household. There is a chance of a good relationship for this couple if they happen to have different interests and are prepared to respect each other's activities in their particular fields.

However, in this case other elements of handwriting will indicate to us this couple's interests and way of thinking. Usually he is more precise in technical aspects, and she will be better at picking up social communication signals. The wife needs the husband's help when she is choosing the fridge, car and even the itinerary of their foreign travels. He will ask her for help in the situation when he wants to ask for a raise, and doesn't know how to go about it. He suggests that she should choose the colour of the car etc.

Of course these examples are descriptions of particular hypothetical cases. We shouldn't define whether or not a relationship is proper solely on the basis of a single feature, namely the slope of the handwriting.

And now, look . . ." he said, rising from the armchair and approaching the shelves with his books on. There were doors on the upper part of the shelves. He opened them and took down a cardboard box, "I have here a few dozen samples of handwriting with variously-sloping letters."

He gave me the box, in which were at least several tens of assorted handwritten pages.

"A good way to learn graphology is an exercise consisting of selecting samples from those letters that you consider the most characteristic and at the beginning studying them very closely. You can, or even should, use the magnifying glass which you have already bought.

Next, trace the samples with a blunt pencil or pointed stick, carefully following the lines of the chosen letters, trying to put yourself into the feelings of the authors."

Saying this, he gave me a pointed stick like a pencil.

Once again, I returned home late. On this occasion, these exercises felt very strange to me. However, during the first hour, which I spent tracing other people's handwriting under the professor's eye, I began to identify with the authors. Perhaps I wasn't yet able to name very well the emotions and associations arising within me, but after strong concentration on the task, I clearly felt the changes of mood associated with the writing style. Step by step the mysterious path to graphology unfolded before me and it was by no means (as I previously thought) the discovery of a magical spell, but the science of penetrating observation and the skill of logically connecting features with images of human personality.

CHAPTER III

TRICHOTOMY

This time we started learning after returning from a walk. The teacher liked to feed the birds in the park, crumbling bread, often while advocating an intriguing thought or sharing interesting facts from various unrelated fields.

More and more I liked and admired the old man.

"In two or three days the rain will fall long and hard, perhaps even for a few days." he said, when we returned to his apartment.

"Why, Professor, when today is so beautiful and the sky is clear?"

"Do you see the clouds over us?" he asked, pointing to the sky.

"They are almost transparent, they're called cirrus. Today, they resemble little rollers or waves like in the sea. Look at them carefully, and you will see that these clouds are hooked at one end. These clouds are many kilometres above us, and there is a change in the position of an atmospheric front, which soon will reach us. As you can see, even from 'cloud handwriting' you can guess the character of the weather."

Once more he astonished me. But I would try to remember what I heard, and I'd check, just on the off chance that rain would fall. We reached his apartment. The lesson began, when he finished feeding the fish swimming in an indoor aquarium. In the meantime, he gave me a piece of paper lying on the desk.

"Look Mark, each element of the triple division of writing, is like an enrichment of the symbolic image of the division of intersubjective psychospace (*Fig. 1*), and here we also find a lot of very interesting references and analogies associated with the significance of space in our perception of reality.

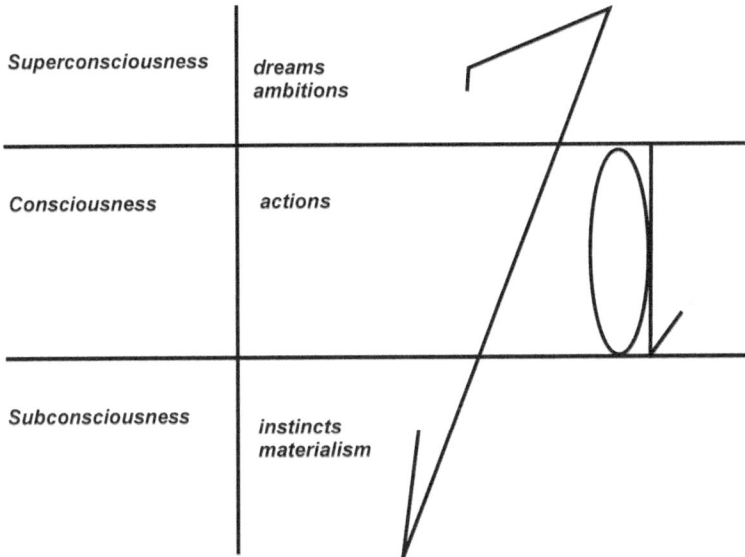

Superconsciousness	*dreams* *ambitions*
Consciousness	*actions*
Subconsciousness	*instincts* *materialism*

Fig. 8. The symbology of triple division of letters

The upper part of the figure:
is at the level of the upper parts of the letters, it means super-consciousness, and corresponds symbolically to the area of ambitions and desires. It is thinking about the future, setting up for development. It symbolises dreams and hopes. I define this part of the letters as the upper accents of the handwriting.

The centre part of the figure:
in the zone marked as consciousness, I have put the central part of letters know by handwriting experts as the ribbon, or track. It is determined primarily on the basis of behaviour and the conscious realisation of one's own 'I' in life. It suggests the typical behaviour and conduct in everyday life. It determines the primary means of communication with other people, and the relationship of the writer to people and the external world. Based on the appearance of the individual elements of the ribbon, a graphologist can determine, in the case of HR consultation, whether the author of the manuscript is suitable for work in a team, or is a confrontational person etc.

The lower part of the figure:
that is accents of the lower letters, the symbolic subconscious. On the basis of analysis of this part of the letter we define mainly attitudes toward sex

and the ability to acquire and use material goods. The basic principle here is the formula which says that the more developed are the below-line elements, this person is more sensual and functions better in life. On the basis of the below-line elements, the graphologist sets out the main components of the future prognosis for potential coexistence of married couples (bearing in mind that a successful sex life cements the relationship).

The most convenient method is to compare the length of the lower and upper accents, depending on the height of the ribbon. The standard is considered to be a ratio of about 1:1:1. This means that, for example, the letter 'o' should lie between the above-line and below-line elements."

"Excuse me, but again I don't really understand what's going on."

"Wait a moment, while I find a diagram that illustrates it well."

He stood, walked over to the desk and for a moment looked through the contents of a drawer. Returning, he began to explain a figure which I was able to catch after just a moment.

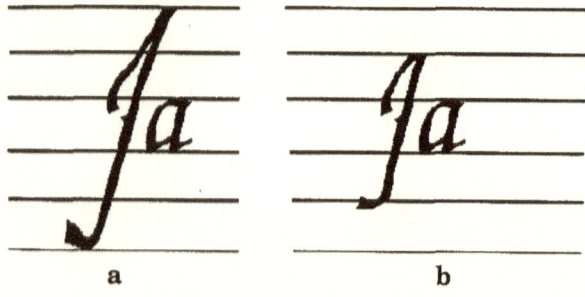

a   b

Fig. 9 Variable length accents

"**In figure a:** you see that the above-line elements are each twice the size of the ribbon. Similarly, the elements below the line are twice as long as the ribbon. Even with such modest information we can guess the greater ambition and sensuality of the text's author.

The adjacent figure: shows the proportion of the accepted norm."

"But how very straightforward it is!" I exclaimed.

"Indeed, the principle is simple, but I suggest you don't generalise too hastily. There are a lot of pitfalls along the way in the interpretation of letters.

Think about how important consequences flow from this interpretation of the above- and below-line elements and the ribbon. The basics are the most important, and thus the subconscious."

"So, the below-line elements?"

"That's right. In relationships, too much difference in the proportions of the below-line elements between the man and the woman usually signifies trouble."

"Why, Professor?"

"It's very possible that one of the two, having significantly longer lower accents, must suppress their sexual capabilities. They possibly discharge their needs in other ways, for example by throwing themselves into their career, or maintaining intimate contact in an additional relationship."

"How can they relieve their sexual tension at work?"

"Because increased sensuality is closely linked to increased sensitivity to the material elements of life such as good wine, a comfortable bed, an elegant car. People with increased sensuality feel the need to make a career, spending money on pleasure, or attaining status. Often, longer below-line elements, highlighted by other features suggest that the person who wrote the letter takes almost physical pleasure in the acquisition of authority and the creation of their own power. Often these people deliberately resign from love in favour of subsequent erotic adventures that cater to their vanity, helping to strengthen their position and not to lessen their activity."

"Do the same things apply to the above-line elements in the handwriting of the partners?"

"No. Talking about the basis, or foundations of relationships, they should be of similar strength. Therefore, in the sphere of upper consciousness even significant differences are the elements which strengthen and cement the relationship."

"I'm sorry, but again I don't know why?"

"Because, when one of the partners has more developed above-line elements, which is ambition or they are a dreamer, then the partner having a bigger ribbon is taking care of everyday matters, and has a superior grasp of reality. Each of the sides learns something from the other. Also it sometimes happens that having a clear difference between the various elements of character, that a man having great ambition can not stand living with someone too mundane. There can also be the opposite situation, where someone 'with their feet on the ground' has had enough of babysitting and caring for the other side representing dreams and unrealistic ideas.

Also in this case, one must remember that one feature is not enough to be sure about your interpretation. Other features of handwriting should reassure us in the interpretation or let us dismiss our theory.

Let's return to the higher above- and below-line elements, and ribbons.

Large upper accents:

if someone in the midst of a peaceful crowd of people jumps up and down, waving his arms in the air, it means that he wants to be noticed.
He wishes to stand out from the crowd.

That's why a large upper accent indicates ambitious, hugely successful people, often seeking power and prestige—sometimes, depending on their shape, dreamers and free spirits.

Excessive prominence of above-line elements indicates to us that the author of the text may be overly ambitious. In connection with other graphological features it can inform us of fanatical interest in religion or any other idea.

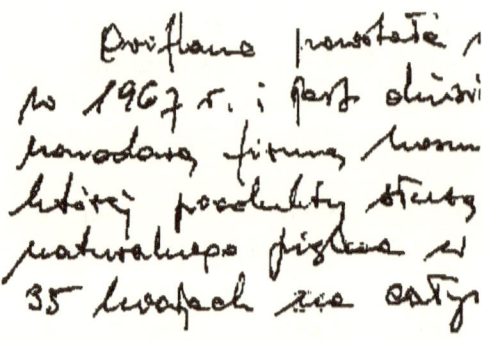

Fig. 10 Large upper accents

Large lower accents:

a tree with strong roots can withstand drought, because it reaches deeper and draws water from there to survive.

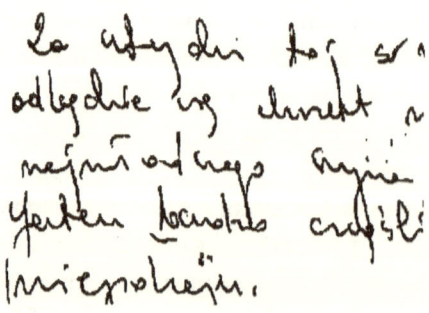

Fig. 11 Large lower accents

Large lower accents of letters suggest great internal strength plus ability to cope with life against adversity, in its practical aspects. It occurs in people who are able to earn a lot of money. Those people also have greater sexual potency, but if it is fully implemented, we will talk about it more in the course of discussing the shape of below-line letter elements.

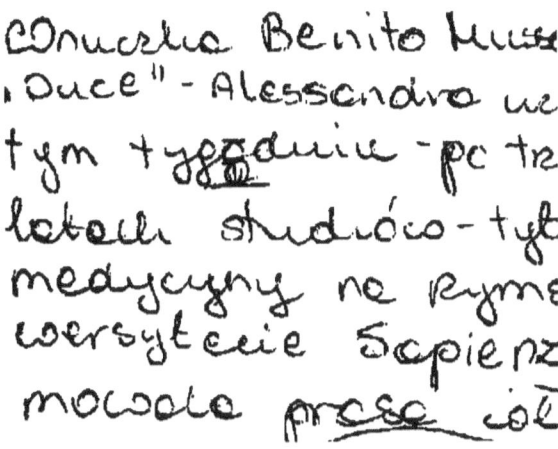

Fig. 12 Large central part (ribbon)

Large ribbon:
When we are aware that time is passing by and the seasons of the year are following, as a prudent person we're always on the move, stocking up in preparation for difficult times, we sort the stores we have gathered so that they can be maximally utilised.

A large ribbon in a letter usually tells us that the writer of the letter is a decisive, bold and enterprising person. He is concentrated mainly on an active life. He rather doesn't philosophise, among occupations he chooses one that allows him to be important and high-profile, and at the same time well-rewarded. A large ribbon is usually associated with another graphological feature, which is big letters. That's why the features of big handwriting and large ribbons are very similar.

A further very important element in the graphological interpretation of handwriting is the analysis of the shape of the letter and other graphic features. As you know, graphology is generally based on analysis of the spatial and symbolic layout of the handwriting, and practically all of its features which deviate from the norm. A graphologist views writing as a record according to certain norms, and exceptions are subject to analysis and interpretation. The way in which we write is like a fingerprint, our personality standing out from among many others. What's more, our handwriting is, at its core, a constant throughout our entire lives. Do you know that people who were injured during the second world war, relearning how to write from the beginning, held their writing tools in their mouths or toes, and after mastering it they wrote with the same handwriting characteristics as before their injuries?"

"How is that possible?"

"Handwriting depicts our inner being, from which there is no way to escape, so a lot of mental illnesses and physical ailments, such as problems with blood circulation, can be determined by graphological analysis."

"I can't wait until I know everything! Could you tell me how long one has to learn in order to be a good graphologist?"

"How good? I don't know what you mean by the expression 'a good graphologist'"

"Well, such as yourself, Professor."

"I have been occupied with graphology for twenty-seven years and I'm still learning something new."

"That means that in twenty-seven years I will be able to understand what handwriting is saying? It's scary."

"I can teach you the basics in a shorter time, you are a very talented young man, the rest you'll have to learn through practice. Fairly soon you will start to draw the correct conclusions through handwriting analysis, and will impress your acquaintances with their accuracy. However, if graphology engages you, it will be with pleasure that you begin to analyse various handwritings, and learn more and more. And now, I'm sorry, I'm tired. I hope that you learned something today."

In the course of the afternoon my world had pretty much turned upside down, I learned to observe from the perspective of the universe. I'm already wondering about what we're going to learn next time. I was also proud of myself because I learned today, incidentally, that I'm potentially a good lover. I felt more confident, but not completely. The word 'potentially' unsettled me, and somehow I didn't dare to ask what it really means.

When I went out into the street it was already dark, and the streetlights alternately lengthened and shortened my shadow on the way home. Sometimes the shadows from two adjacent lamps would partially overlap. One was usually longer for a moment and shortened as I approached one of the lamps, and when I passed, it lengthened while the neighbouring lamp placed its shadow, much longer and less visible. Each of them was a shadow of my figure, the same figure despite the differences, and each enriched my picture, drawing me at the same time a little differently. I looked at the sky and thought that I need to learn to observe from the earth's perspective, before trying that of the cosmos.

CHAPTER IV

HANDWRITING SIZE

"Will you drink tea, Mark?"

"Yes please!"

The clatter of the dishes accompanied his voice coming from the kitchen. The window was ajar, and the wind coming into the room was playing with the curtains. It was a Sunday, so the noise of the traffic coming in through the open window was not particularly persistent. Despite the hot summer days, it remained pleasantly cool in the room, the old thick walls of the building protected well against the heat of the day.

"As you have surely noticed, we aren't talking about the history of graphology. If you're interested, help yourself to graphology books, and it's summarised in each.

You should note however, that this knowledge has been built by many generations of eminent graphologists and is not a closed subject, despite the wealth of information already collected.

It's therefore worth mentioning a few names. The father of modern graphology is Jean Hyppolyte Michoń, a monk. He built the foundations of the French, and with it the global school of graphology.

He published the first significant book in this field in as early as 1872.

In Germany, graphology has developed very rapidly, and there its precursor and creator of the whole school was a German psychologist Ludwig Klages.

In Poland, the only world-renowned figure was Raphael Schermann. He laid the foundations of the so-called symbolism of psychospace, which you have just learned. He was, however, more clairvoyant than graphologist. He pointed out that a person symbolically and unconsciously creates a graphic image of their character and dreams. For example, one who dreams of flying possesses a signature in the shape of a propeller, while the potential suicide has a signature the shape of a pistol. He was never mistaken in his interpretations, but others wishing to follow him on the basis of his instructions were frequently wrong. It was only the following generation of Polish handwriting experts, focussing on symbolism, who developed his concepts.

Another prominent Polish graphologist was active at the same time in Poznań, then Henryk Gralski-Grudzinski in Kraków, who developed the 'graphological key', a technique for interpreting handwriting based on his own extended methods of the innovative concepts of Klages. Gralski was also the founder in 1923 of the Institute of Scientific Graphology, and one of his students is preparing to publish a book on the subject of Professor Gralski's graphological method.

As you know, WWII and the period thereafter in Poland was not conducive to any freethinkers, and this included psychographologists. Especially in the period up to Stalin's death, in all countries controlled by the Soviet Union, it was not permitted to have one's own views. My teacher told me about graphology in great secrecy; he was already very old and in a great hurry. To this day I don't understand why he chose me. I also don't know how it happened that I, a young proud member of a youth organisation, ready to defend the life of the socialist fatherland against the depredations of imperialism, began with great enthusiasm to learn prohibited graphology. They were very strange times. I too am already not one of the youngest . . ."

"Oh please, Professor!?"

"Yes, you're right."

He frightened me with these words, and at the same time treated me as a partner, told me today a piece of his own history, but I couldn't really think about his words as he took a sip of his weak tea with lemon and continued.

"Returning to our classes Mark, as we have already noticed, it is very important to get to know a certain interpretative key to our subconscious perceptions of the world, which are also used in the work of the graphologist. A main graphological principle is the use in handwriting analysis of an informed knowledge of symbols and in the aspect of line and space, about which I spoke to you before. Handwriting is an excellent record of thinking in a linear fashion, i.e. from—to, in which symbolic references are skillfully combined. Every form of communication is symbolic communication. When writing any sentence we cannot simultaneously give up all of our thoughts. We can, however, record them in sequence. On the other hand each word is nothing more than a symbol and we can analyse it symbolically, that is to say multidimensionally."

"Could you explain that to me, Professor? I guess once again I don't really understand."

"Besides the impact of the symbol in relation to space, there are a number of other analogies related to power and gender. For example largeness is a man's feature, and smallness is inextricably linked to femininity and delicacy.

Largeness is also:
being pushy, external, gawky, showy, strong, dominant and overwhelming.

Smallness is:
modest, inconspicuous, tractable, gentle, internal, hidden and timid. You've surely noticed that the terms I mentioned do not contradict each other. Furthermore, in our feelings they complement each other. In reality this is still a continuation of spatial thinking. If you remember, on the right we set the male features, and on the left, the female.

Left side	Right side
femininity	*masculinity*
interior	*determination*
weakness	*strength*
delicacy	*gawky*
home	*large*
mystery	*extravagance*
complexity	*simplicity*

Fig. 13 Terms associated with the left and right sides

Therefore someone who writes with large letters is usually a dynamic person, who likes to be important and fills their personal space, not only on paper but their living space.

Businessmen, politicians, artists, people who hold public office, usually write with large letters.

Large letters—also associated with greater passion, courage, pugnacity. Many leaders wrote with large letters. Large letters may also indicate superstition, arrogance and authoritarianism."

"Does that mean that anyone who writes with big letters has such a character?"

"Yes, but if other elements of the handwriting will indicate suppression of features typical of people writing with large letters, these features do not show themselves as strongly as in clearer instances of handwriting. But, you already know about the slope of the letters from our earlier lesson.

If we combine letters in a manuscript sloping to the left with large handwriting, it gives rise to the conclusion that we are dealing with a person who is more cautious in their actions and self-centered, but still craving importance and recognition.

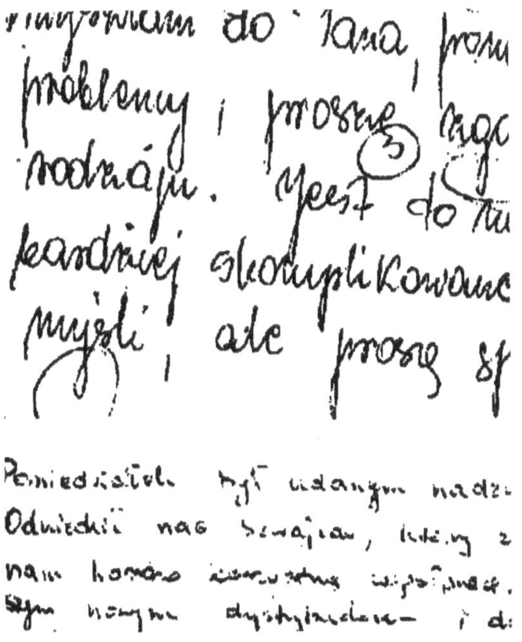

Fig. 14 Small and large handwriting

You will learn about the other characteristic features one by one in the course of further study.

To graphologists the size of the letter, which they consider large or small, they give in millimetres measured at the height of the ribbon. For this measurement letters of the type n, o, c or a are used. I don't want you to rely on the dimensions given in millimetres, because at this stage of your education you should rely only on the main and distinct characters of the handwriting. For the record however, I'll tell you that a large letter is one whose ribbon height exceeds 4.5-5 mm.

Small letters are those the size of whose ribbon is no more than 2.5 mm. When you are in doubt into which group you should qualify the handwriting size, it is better to omit this feature, focussing on other elements of the handwriting. The best thing to do when analysing text for the features of large or small handwriting is to qualify such handwriting that you see without a shadow doubt is clearly standing out from the norm. I assure you that in this case you will not make a mistake.

We will also not analyse a ribbon of average size on the grounds that it is of typical width. In order to perform a good analysis a graphologist looks for deviations from the norm. We will skip typical elements as less important, since they can be defined as average and typical of the majority.

Small handwriting:
indicates a rather more modest person, insecure, introverted in behaviour and cautious. Usually they are more reasonable, critical and shy. People writing with smaller letters are better able to focus on details and are more interested in technology, architecture, mathematics etc.

Handwriting with variable-sized letters:
signifies troubled people. They wish to rise above mediocrity in life. Such states of internal stress often suggest large ambitions and a disturbed inner balance. Often people who write in this way are searching for something, creative and artistically talented. after all, a typical feature of a creator is his internal unrest."

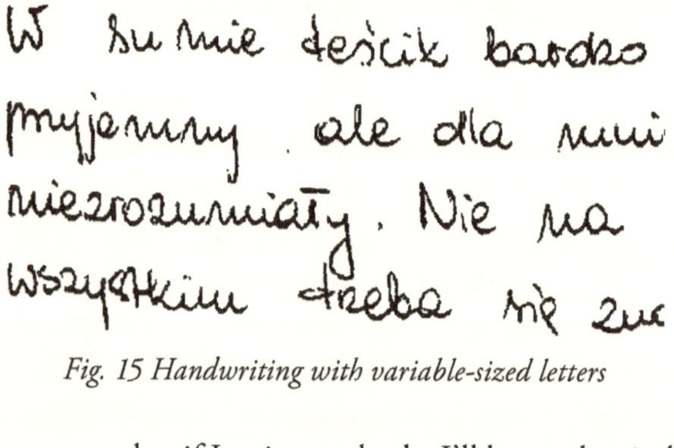

Fig. 15 Handwriting with variable-sized letters

"Does that mean that if I write carelessly, I'll be careless in life?"

"Yes. I see that you are beginning to think like a graphologist, and after such a short time of studying! I'm proud of you Mark, very few people understand these principles so quickly.

If the handwriting is slapdash, it reveals itself also in domestic tasks such as cleaning, cooking, hygiene, or even in choosing friends, or looking after your own car. This is on condition however, that other handwriting features don't show us the existence of other areas to which the author pays more attention. Often, staying with your comparison, carelessness in handwriting becomes apparent at the end of the line. Such a record informs us of lack of discipline and of care in the longer term. Someone who writes like this will be trying to work hard, and will even give a very good first impression, but will have a lot of difficulty maintaining this impression. It may also be that the author became tired while writing.

The size of the letters is also an essential element in the comparative analysis of handwriting. **When both partners in a relationship have large handwriting**, this is not a favourable union. Each will want to lead and to have the final word in all matters. At each step, partners with letters approaching equal size, if they are big, will struggle for power. It may resemble an officer who expresses astonishment that his subordinate not only did not listen to his orders, but tried to give his own.

When both partners write with small letters, and when the angle of the handwriting is the same, there is often not a more proactive, decisive person, who will determine a course of action in life.

The most favourable condition between partners in business or personal relationships seems to be a union in which the sizes of the handwriting are clearly different.

At the end of this part of the lesson I wish to remind you that you should very carefully observe the changes in the handwriting which are happening at the time. After all, there may often be a gradual or sudden change in the size of the letters, depending on whether it is the beginning of the writing, or we are analysing the last words of a manuscript.

Larger handwriting at the beginning of a page:
is interpreted as boldness and initiative-taking at the beginning of a relationship. In the course of getting to know one another more closely, a person with this kind of writing becomes more modest, and less decisive in action than would follow from their earlier behaviour.

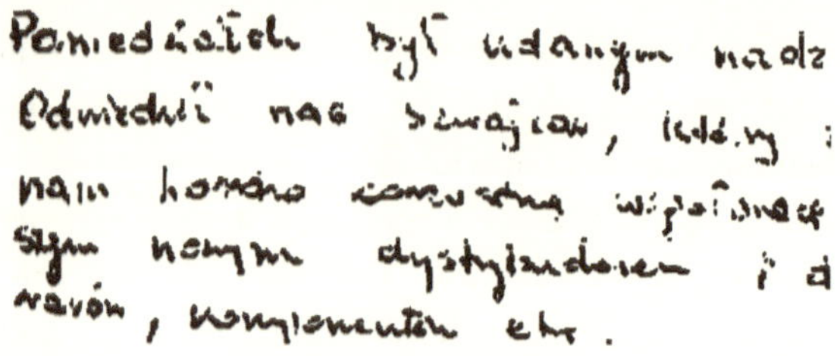

Fig. 16 Larger handwriting at the beginning of the page

In some cases, there may be presumed to be greater caution in action and the desire to sort out one's life due to troubles arising in connection with over-bold action earlier in life.

Smaller handwriting at the beginning of a page:
is interpreted as modesty and timidity at the beginning of knowing someone, but that after familiarisation with the people and the situation, the person writing this way became bolder and more initiative-taking in action. And, in this case it can also be presumed, a situation in which the writer became bolder after an earlier period of suppression of their personality and being in an environment in which they were dominated. The particular case of enlargement of letters in handwriting is writing larger the first letter on the page.

This is interpreted by handwriting experts mainly as a desire to impress and make an impact on the environment at first contact. People who emphasise the first letter of their writing often arrive late at parties, in order to stand out more. They behave loudly and nonchalantly. They like it when everyone's attention is focussed entirely on them. In contact with other people they try to be unconventional, to strike people with their originality in outlook and behaviour.

At this moment we should mention another important detail.

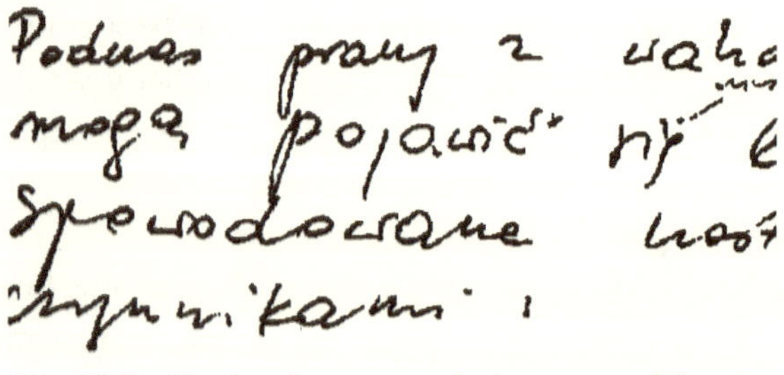

Fig. 17 Smaller handwriting at the beginning of the page

Writing the first letter separately from the text:
I have in my mind a tiny separation of the first letter from the rest of the word. Such writing is interpreted as action after thought. Movement of the hand paused for a moment during writing, and restarted in a different place. In life, the meaning of this symbol is very similar. It is explained as restarting an action after a moment of reflection, and continuing it, but possibly with a slightly different attitude. We create a similar interpretation, somewhat akin to the case of large handwriting, in relation to wide handwriting.

Wide handwriting:
is also symbolic of letters jostling for position in the line and is typical of pushy and short-tempered people. Wide handwriting also means a dynamic and optimistic attitude to life, creative and decisive in action. A person with wide handwriting is open-handed and worldly-wise, and would like to be influential on the larger stage."

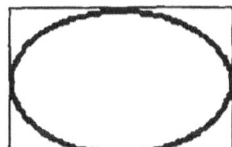 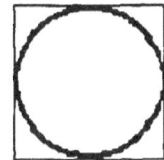 

Fig. 18 The letter 'o' in various widths

"Excuse me, but I don't know how to measure the width of handwriting. Does a method exist to make letter width measurement easier?"

"Of course, there is a very simple method. Usually, a square is taken as a norm in which may be written the letters: n, o, e. If the base is wider than the side of the rectangle then we are dealing with wide letters. The base can be narrower than the side of the rectangle, and in this case we are dealing with narrow handwriting. On this occasion I have prepared a diagram which will make it easier for you to understand this subject.

Narrow handwriting:
As you would probably suspect, it should be interpreted as unwillingness to stand out; Low dynamism, fear of action, internal unsureness. It's a kind of constraint of the letters in the course of writing which is similar to a person constrained in action and in thought.

Of course, on the subject of handwriting width, we can have changes over time. We interpret it differently depending on the way in which the handwriting width changes.

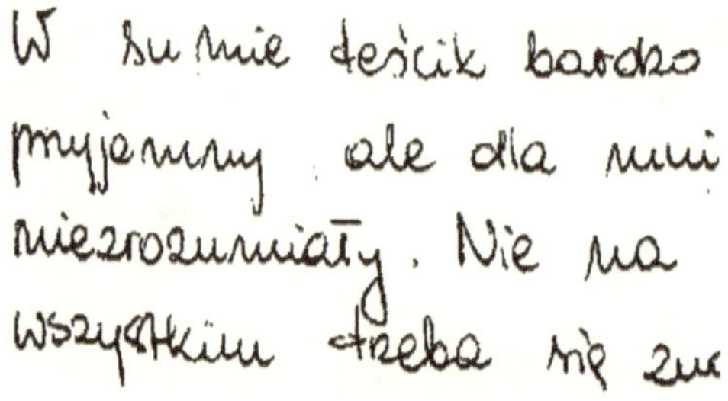

Fig. 19 Wide handwriting

Wide handwriting at the beginning of the page:
In graphological analysis it is interpreted as increased dynamism, initiative and optimism in action, which have arisen from the trials and tribulations of life. In consequence a person who writes in this way may react vigorously to suggestions and ideas, however after a certain time will become more cautious and suppress their emotions.

This reflects suppression of emotions and their own expression in actions at the beginning of tasks. Whereas, later on there ensues an increased involvement in dynamism and optimism during action.

At the end of this chapter in the field of psychographology, I would like to remind you once again that you should not draw your conclusions too hastily. Features related to size about which we were talking, should be confirmed by other graphological features."

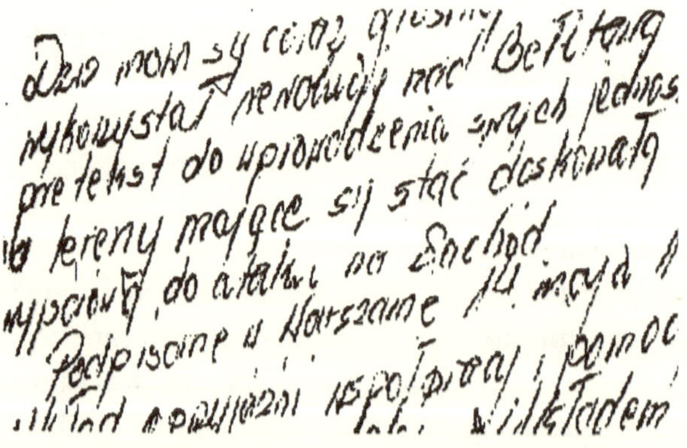

Fig. 20 Example of narrow handwriting

In the evening, looking through the window of my room, and observing the flickering lights of the city at night, I was analysing the lesson of the day. I was reminded of an article in which the author drew attention to the fact that the size of a car can be related to the feeling of internal strength. A pedestrian always feels psychologically at a disadvantage compared to a motorist, and the owner driving his car has a more dismissive attitude to the pedestrian. Drivers of large vehicles feel that they are the most important road-users. Drivers of personal cars prefer to give way to bigger vehicles just in case. I noticed also that politicians have big cars, big suitcases, big plans and ambitions, big desks. so their big handwriting is not a coincidence.

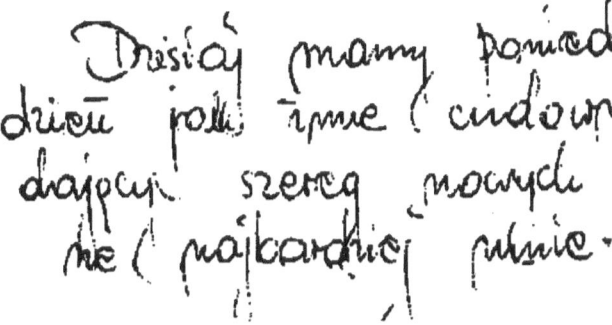

Fig. 21 Unduly large letters beginning the page

CHAPTER V

HANDWRITING PRESSURE

The professor went over to the window and stared straight ahead through it for a long while.

"Come over here for a moment, Mark." When I stood beside him, he pointed to the park across the street and asked "Do you see that sudden drop in the level of the ground in the park across the street? It stretches right to the centre of the town and along that hollow where there are unusual hillocks?"

Indeed, in the farther part of the park the land rapidly dropped but after a moment rose steeply. I knew that this depression ran the length of the park and continued through the town several kilometres deep.

"Yes, I can see it, is there something wrong with it?" I asked, not knowing what was going on.

"Here, a long time ago was a glacier, a huge several-hundred kilometre mass of ice pushing ahead of itself a rampart of boulders. Surely you learned about it. This that you can see is the remains of the bottom of the moraine. Under the base of the glacier the strength of its pressure created this formation. The earth buckled tighter here under its weight. The glacier departed, but it left its mark."

"I didn't know." In fact I didn't know where he was heading.

"Everything leaves its mark, one more visible, another less. The durability of a track depends on the force that made it. The force can be social, cultural, scientific, technical and, as in the case of this glacier, physical. The more you influence the environment the longer-lasting is the mark. It's the same with handwriting. A person also writes depending on personality with greater or less force.

Handwriting force:
is a form of reinforcing the meaning of interpretation of handwriting features. As you no doubt remember, at the beginning of our lessons we

spoke about spatial symbolism. We talked of the meaning of the right side as stronger and the left as the weaker. The force of the handwriting is strongly associated with those terms.

Strong force:
reinforces the intensity of all the graphological handwriting features that indicate strength, such as handwriting leaning to the right, big letters, wide letters, angular letters, which we will talk about a little later. Generally, strong force emphasises dynamism in action and great psychological strength. It also informs us of high sensuality and independence in action, and emphasises aggression.

If, for example, handwriting is sloping to the right, you surely remember that we defined it as typical of a man of action. If additionally there is strong force in this handwriting we interpret it as even more decisive in action. If the handwriting is big, with greater force, this means a higher wish to be dominant, and to stand out."

"But how can you recognize that the force is strong or weak?"

"The simplest method, quite sufficient for our needs, is analysis by turning over the piece of the paper that the handwriting is on. You notice that on the other side there is an imprint of the handwriting. If the imprint is visible, that means that the force was strong, since the pen left a clear trace on the paper. To be able to estimate the level of the force you should practise at home, how to make a trace on the paper, also depending on the type of surface, because the imprint looks different when the text is written in an exercise book, to when it is written on a single piece of paper on a hard surface, for example on a marble- or glass-topped table.

Very strong force:
leaving on the paper a trace so deep that it causes a cutting into the paper usually suggests very strong psychological disorders and disorders in coordination of movement."

"Indeed, this is very logical and straightforward" I added, for the sake of saying something, angry with myself that I didn't catch this before.

"Weak force:
when handwriting doesn't leave any trace on the other side of the paper. It is interpreted as a sign of a weaker physical condition, bigger imagination and

smaller strength of will. Additionally it indicates less perseverance and an increased susceptibility to influence.

In our spatial symbolism it diminishes the strength of the right-side graphological elements such as large letters, leaning to the right etc. Whereas it enhances the strength of the other, weaker graphological elements such as small letters, leaning to the left, or ornamental flourishes, about which we will talk more in a while."

"May I in this case ask for an example?"

"Small handwriting indicated modesty, meticulousness and cautiousness in actions. Combined with weak force those features become stronger. Someone writing this way is even more cautious and meticulous and suggests even more someone who is overtired or having very weak physical condition.

Variable force:

is typical of people of unstable mood. They are easily excited by new ideas, but before they finish them they fall into apathy and boredom, and very quickly moving on to the next idea. They can have difficulty with concentration. Often their instability and lack of willpower causes conflict within their social environment.

It's good to train our own force, in order to form our own opinions about imprints on the other side of the paper, depending on the force used and the choice of writing implement. writing with a fountain pen we cannot press with too strong a force against the paper on account of the delicacy of the tool.

By chance we have touched on a rather important matter in graphological analysis, which we did not speak about earlier, which is also the choice of the writing tool by the author of the handwriting.

Those who write with a fountain pen:

are usually people of a higher cultural level, by nature traditionalists, cleaving to cultural forms and adhering to universally accepted ethical standards. They like beauty, often they escape to their own dream world. A very expensive fountain pens is a synonym of wealth, luxury and the refined tastes of the pen's owner. However, too shiny and flashy in form or colour, demonstrates snobbishness and doing things for show.

Those who write with a fine line pen:

For mentally weak people, internally unsure, with weaker combative spirit, a fine line pen for taking notes is a common attribute of their internal dilemmas. The fact that they have this wonderful tool gives them hope that their spiritual dilemma will go unseen. The fine line pen has this advantage, that however strongly you press on the surface, the width of the lines is unchanged. It looks like the trace of strong, even writing.

Those who write with a ballpoint pen:
The ballpoint pen has become the standard, which is why we analyse the graphological features, and we ignore the fact that it has been written with a ballpoint pen.

And now I suggest that we take a short break."

After this portion of the lecture we went together for a walk. The reason for this was that the teacher wanted to buy some mint sweets. He explained to me that he knew how bad smoking was for him, nevertheless he bought cigarettes. It's strange, but he never smoked in front of me.

Actually, I don't know anything about him. I have the impression that he tried not to show me his weaknesses. I was already a little accustomed to his personality and it seemed to me that I could recognize when he felt bad. I didn't see any photos in his flat. I didn't know if he had any family. Even when he didn't feel well, I saw a rebellious expression, he was still fighting, struggling with himself and probably the whole world. It reminded me of how he spoke to me.

"Remember, my boy, search for your own truth and the path to it. When you are much older, it may be that you will discover that many people, even with scientific titles will argue with your beliefs, having no scientific arguments to confirm their thesis. They will be the office-boys of science, because a scientist is one who seeks the truth and has the boldness to ask uncomfortable questions. The wise person doesn't laugh at any concept, they perhaps only claim that they have no evidence with which to confirm it. Often, a theme mocked by the office-boys of science is astrology. I don't know for sure if a correlation exists between our birth and character, and the arrangement of celestial bodies. However I know that it was worked on by Copernicus, Kepler and Newton. I don't take them for fools, I'm convinced that they saw important reasons for working on it."

"I didn't think about it in this way, rather that this was silliness."

"You may assert this, if you check. But I'm not surprised that you think this way. There exists in our country a kind of scientific censure, which not only suppresses knowledge, but also hides and distorts the important facts from history, which are nowadays uncomfortable. Very interesting for me is the fact that young people are not informed that Newton was not a physicist."

"What?!"

"For thirty years he had been working on something that we commonly call magic—he was the greatest magician in the Europe of those times. The law of gravity he discovered as a consequence of his deliberations that were deeper and wider than those to which he is currently assigned. I don't agree with the definition of him as an outstanding thinker in one area and the concealment of his work in other areas less comfortable for modern science.

It seems to me that it doesn't detract from the value of the discovery, made by Copernicus, of the fact that a contribution to the consideration of whether the geocentric planetary system was correct, was that it was a very inelegant way of explaining retrogradation."

I admit that I didn't know what he was talking about. He noticed a look of uncertainty on my face, because he hurried with the explanation.

"Retrogradation is the apparent backward movement of the planets relative to the earth. Copernicus came to the conclusion that only setting the sun as the main celestial body, around which the other planets orbit, could neatly and elegantly explain the retrograde movement of the planets. Of course, retrogradation was a very important element in the interpretation of astrological horoscopes.

CHAPTER VI

THE MEANING OF MARGINS

Each of us develops his own work method, but the initial actions in the analysis of handwriting are common to the majority of graphologists. I also think that many more psychologists will accept graphology in our country as a wonderful method for analysing a person's character, if they would treat it as a further **personality test**. Graphology is a very specific and rich personality test, but from the point of view of symbolic analysis it doesn't differ from the most popular tests used by psychologists. An example may be the **RORSCHACH A** test, **JUCKER's "tree"** test, or **TAT**. Graphology has one undeniable superiority over other personality tests set by psychologists. It is a form of non-invasive test. The person whose handwriting we are testing does not have to know anything about it. Of course this advantage in inappropriate hands can become misuse. Therefore, every graphologist should be characterised by a high sense of responsibility.

Psychographology is used mainly in psychological tests having as their goal finding the reasons for conflicts in relationships, and in searching for the right candidate for responsible positions in work, often only having access to a handwritten CV.

It's also worth mentioning that knowing even the basics of graphology, it isn't possible to change the characteristics of one's handwriting just for the occasion, that is falsifying the picture of one's personality. Every attempt ends up usually changing the slope or size of the letters. A person knowing other personality tests is much more easily able to falsify their results.

It's worth mentioning here that in the case of psychographology there appear other not less striking possibilities, completely unavailable to typical personality tests. Namely, if we suggest to the writer, small and subtle changes in the writing, but I repeat once more, very delicate changes in the handwriting, we can cause changes in the writer's behaviour in the desired direction."

"This almost borders on magic, or something of that nature, Professor."

"No, my boy, this follows from logic, if you think about it. Since each of our behaviours, including handwriting, reflects our internal psychological state, it's obvious that in changing external elements, for instance our own handwriting, we have an influence on our interior. Such therapy is very helpful in cases of sensitivity, especially for children with whom we can inculcate certain elements of handwriting in a different way. Of course we cannot change the character of a person by changing their handwriting; personality seems to be irreformable and we can only slightly change attitude towards life and activate suppressed dynamism and resistance to stress. On the other hand just these tiny changes in attitude towards life are very often the cause of significant changes in their lives.

Returning to the main topic of today's lesson, I repeat that in psychographological analysis, we always start from an analysis of the general filling of the space on the paper and drawing attention to the especially outstanding features of the handwriting. That's why it's very important to me, if someone can divide space in a correct and clear manner. Or if it's all written in one burst without any spaces separating one thought from another. If the author of the handwriting is able to write their thoughts in a clear way, then in action in other fields they will show that they are more organized.

I look for whether handwriting is more or less mature; I define the level of its legibility, following the rule from general to specific."

"Why is it important to keep that order in analysis?"

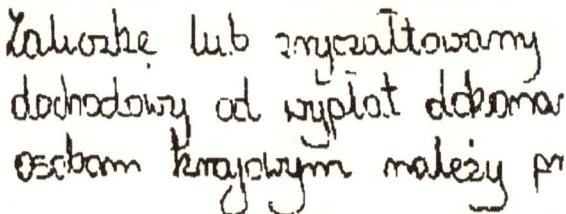

Fig. 22. Immature handwriting of a 35-year old man

"Because, in the first stage of analysis the tiny elements, e.g. features of some letter, can confuse the general characterological picture. A person has such a nature that often being suggested to by the first premise, even one of less importance, loses the objectivity of their opinion. If we begin the analysis from the general handwriting features, we have a greater chance that our analysis will be error-free.

Using the analogy, we can assume that it is significantly easier to fill in the construction, initially sketched in general terms of the contents, than to build arduously from fragments, without marking out the main direction. It would be rather difficult to assemble a jigsaw puzzle without the knowledge that allows us to understand the general picture of the puzzle.

In addition it's never possible to be certain if this which we were able to assemble, and more or less fit together, is correctly connected.

A graphologist searches mostly for traits or such of the characteristics of handwriting that stand out and are exceptional to the generally accepted norms. It's really thanks to those characteristic features that we can distinguish one personality from another. As the name suggests, those features characterise us.

One must also remember that the handwriting of an adult which is the template and almost doesn't depart from school standards, is also a decidedly atypical feature and belongs to the exceptions.

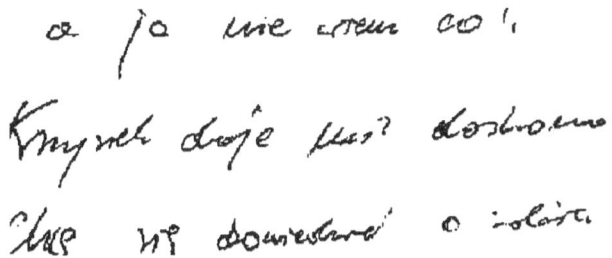

Fig. 23. The mature handwriting of a 25-year-old man

Each of us, despite a common school template, with the passage of time and during the course of development of individual character, slightly changes and simplifies our own handwriting, until the moment when the fully-matured version no longer bears any resemblance to the school pattern from the beginning of education.

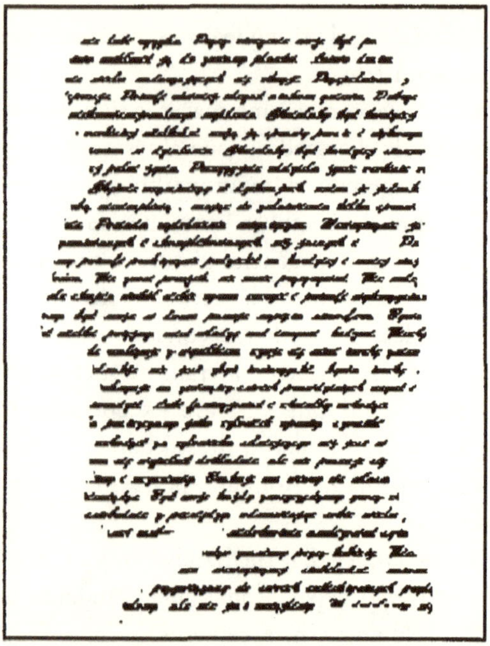

Fig. 24. Front and back handwriting

Our general analysis will develop in the course of our migration through the successive elements, inspecting individual letters. Some of the features will become stronger, others will become weaker or will be admitted conditionally. However, the whole time we can not forget about the general impression.

Pay attention to how the margins are located, what is their width and what shape they have. We must not forget that the margin is the empty space, gap or interval between the handwriting and the edge of the paper. However, the handwriting is always important and for instance the term 'wavy margin' describes a varying, changeable distance of the start of the handwriting relative to the edge of the paper.

Left margins:
are symbolically related to our front, our external behaviour."

"How is that? You said earlier, Professor, that the left side is the symbolic interior." Finally I was able to find an example of the lack of consistency, and illogicality in the lecture; I was proud of myself that I noticed the error.

"In order to explain to you this apparent contradiction I will use a diagram." He was unperturbed.

"So, left margins:

As you can see, handwriting is not only literal, but also a symbolic fulfilment of the contents of the paper. As we fill in the surface of the paper, so we fill in the contents of our life. If we grab the script in our hand, the beginning of the text becomes the left margin;

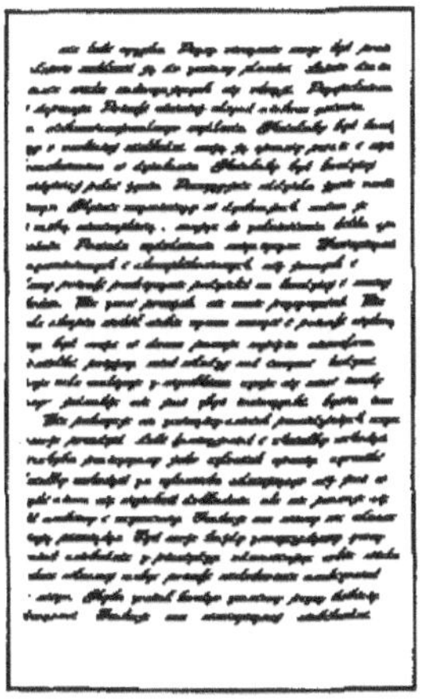

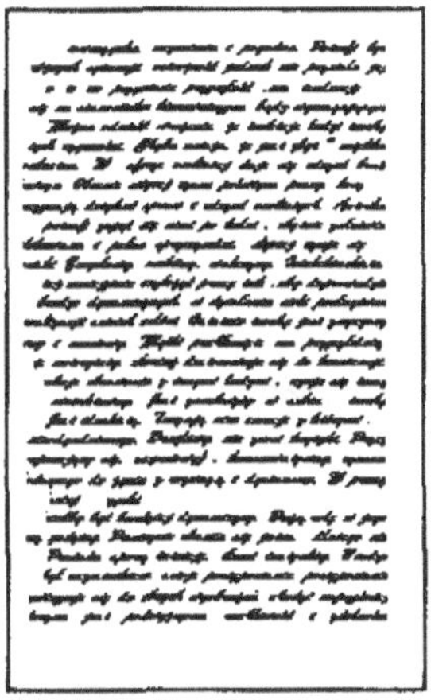

Fig. 25. Straight left margin Fig. 26. Wavy left margin

this is the symbolic face, front, façade, the back of the script is the right margin; it is the internal world, a secret, something hidden inside.

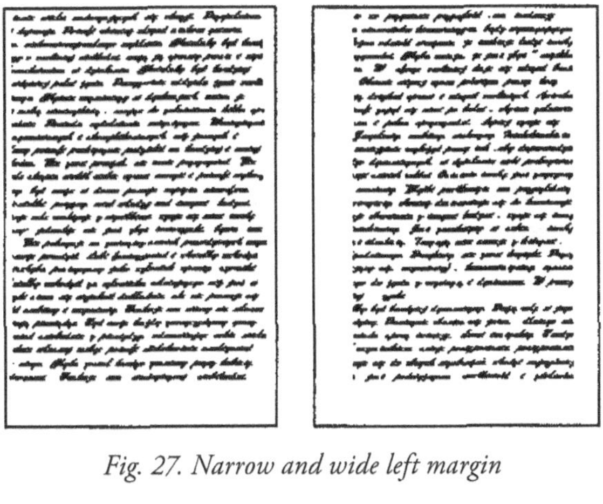

Fig. 27. Narrow and wide left margin

Simply one should remember that the whole front of the handwriting is another quality and has a different reference point to the beginning of a line or paragraph."

"I guess I understand. It's like a fashion designer who can analyse shoes as being high-fashion, or well-designed from the shoe's point of view, but the same shoes are at the same time an important element of a greater whole, which is a style of dress."

"Now I will present you with the symbolic meaning of some of the most frequently appearing types of margins.

Straight left margin:

is written by an ostentatious person, who is able to present themselves externally as strong and stable. A disciplined person, able to maintain a good external image.

Narrow left margin:

is a symbolic hugging of the edge of the page. It symbolises fear, a sense of unsureness, the wish to conceal one's interior from the external world. Sometimes it testifies to excessive thrift or of financial difficulties.

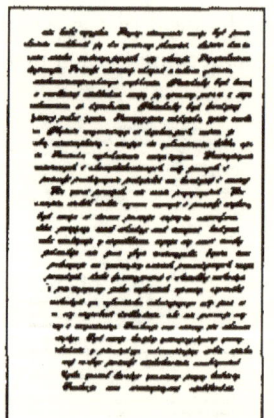 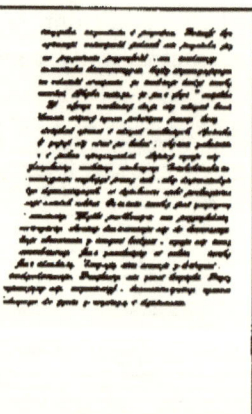

Fig. 28. Widening left margin Fig. 29. Narrowing left margin

Wide left margin:

is the symbolic giving of a space (field) for other people to present themselves. The wide margin is typical of tolerant people, good observers and shy people.

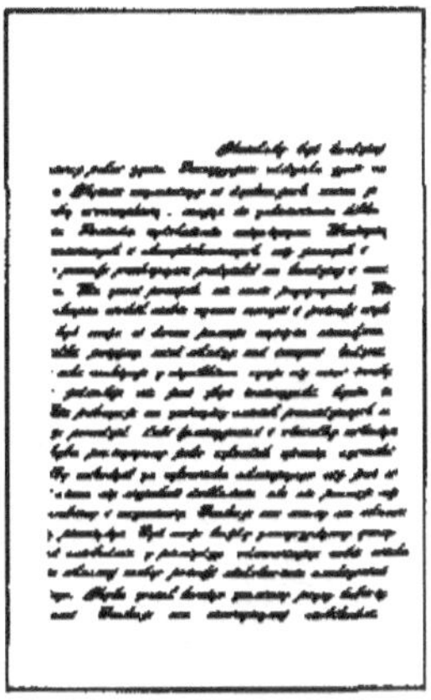

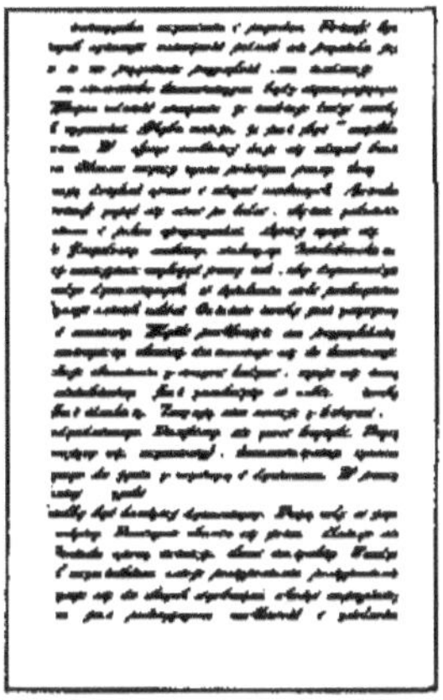

Fig. 30. Wide top margin Fig. 31. Narrow top margin

Wavy left margin:
As with the wavy margin, so is it difficult for the author to maintain their internal image of strength and decisiveness. They are usually abused by others and unable to refuse them favours. This kind of effort increases personal tension and irritability.

Widening left margin:
The more clearly the margin widens, the more the author of the script is wasting the space available for writing. Graphological interpretation defines this feature as symptomatic of wasting money and trouble with saving. Usually, impulsive people write in this way.

Narrowing left margin:
Slightly reminiscent of the script hugging the edge of the paper. This feature is interpreted as a fear of people or financial troubles. Often, fearfulness and pessimism are those invoked by recently undergone problems of a financial nature. Additionally the author of the script perceives the world as sad, grey and full of danger. He is risk-averse, as he doesn't want to be defeated again.

Remembering that since in handwriting we are looking for traits, we can also graphologically interpret the top margin.

Wide top margin:
We interpret this as wanting to yield space to someone more important. The main interpretative feature of such handwriting, is an uncritical acceptance of authority and superiors. Additionally, strong inhibition and low self-esteem.

Narrow top margin, or lack of margin:

This is a clear desire to underline self-esteem and struggle with authority. Actually no boss will be good enough to be fully accepted. Often such writers choose freelancing, or become the boss themselves. They don't leave any space at the top of the page for someone else. Usually they live in a state of tension and are irritable.

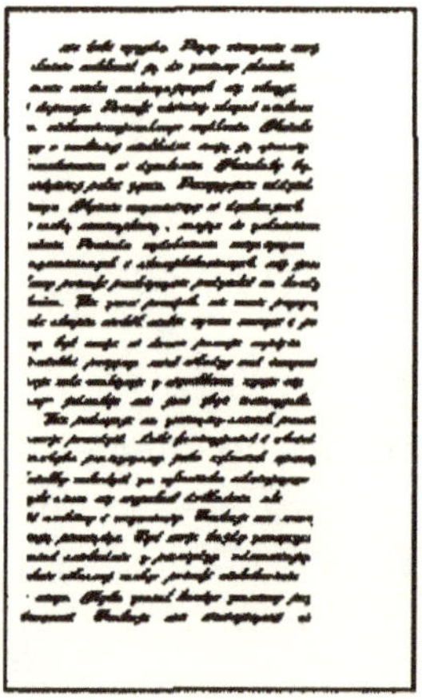

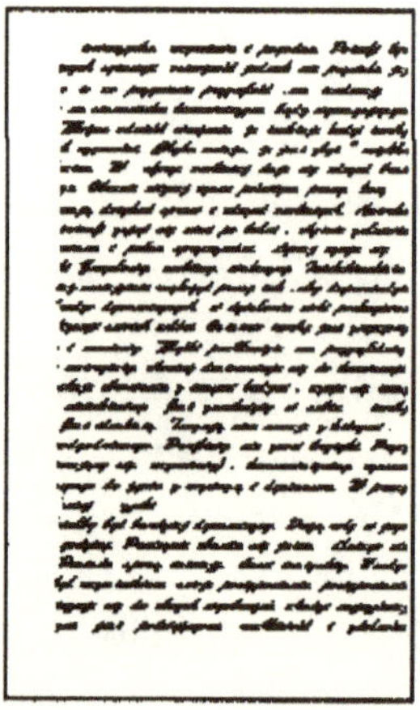

Fig. 32. Wide right margin Fig. 33. Narrow right margin

Wide right margin:

It is a symbolic expression of internal uncertainty and lack confidence in their own abilities. Imagine that the length of the line of handwriting reflects your activity. If you finish it too early, also in life you don't start a lot of things—just in case, on the assumption that what you have actually achieved is sufficient. Those using wide margins present themselves as shy people.

Narrow right margin:

This tells us that someone who writes in this manner pushed a little too far. They crossed certain limits. This is interpreted as having frequent reflections of an existential nature. Thoughts of the type: what is everything for; what is the purpose of life, and suchlike. Such a person can spark off an idea or a work, but when there are obstacles on the road, doubt and apathy appear. They wait, analysing the meaning of life, until the next idea interrupts them.

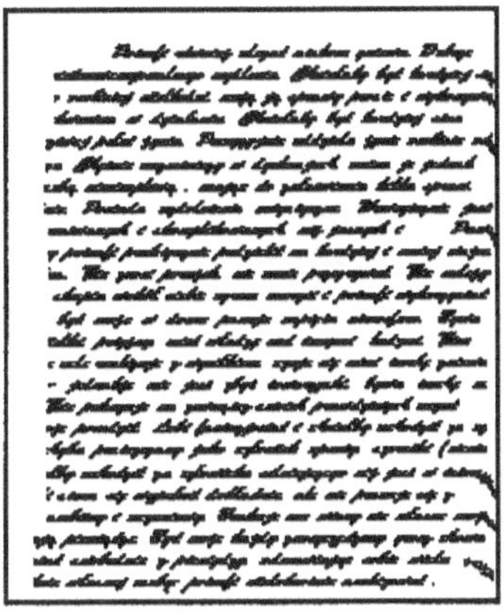

Fig. 34. Right margin falling

Falling line level:

These are a sort of feature reinforcement, related to narrow right margins. They additionally inform us about strong states of depression. If the handwriting doesn't fit to the line and is extended to the edge of the page turning sharply down, it can suggest suicidal thoughts. If we compared the line of handwriting to the line of the lips on a drawing of the human face, it would look exactly like how the corners of the mouth fall in an expression of sorrow and grief.

Remember though, that the sharp fall of the lines is typical of very strong depression. However, someone who has already decided to give up on life is internally quieter, and at the end of the lines of handwriting his script will be more balanced.

Fig. 35. Symbolic shape of the mouth in depression

Straight right margin:

Obviously there is no method of aligning the right margin during the course of writing in the same way as the left. But, the right margin can be more or less consistent. Usually a consistent, aligned right margin is a result of skilful handling of words and correct estimation of the length of the words. Many people aren't able to, or have never tried to rearrange the words in the lines. Skilful word-handling is also skill in handling matters which we cannot finish today and put off until the following day. An aligned, consistent margin indicates internal strength.

Haven't I bored you enough, Mark?"

"Of course not, Professor! I'm busily noting everything down." I admit that I was cold for a moment, when I was hearing about strong depression, concluded from the shape of the lines.

"In that case, we will start our next meeting from the analysis of the information we are given by the various shapes of lines of handwriting."

CHAPTER VII

THE MEANING OF LINES

"Look, Mark, at this lamp that I bought once with great difficulty due to its high price. I was enchanted by its shape." Here, he pointed to probably the only thing that wasn't harsh in appearance. the lamp was standing on his desk—it was indeed beautiful. Made of bronze with a pearly white shade intertwined with threads of the same metal as the base, it seemed airy and fragile.

"It's beautiful and exactly captures the *art nouveau* character of its time. We read a great deal from the shapes of the sculptures, type of clothes, the lines in architecture, about the characteristics of the epoch. They look different, the ascetic forms of sculptures and buildings of the Middle Ages, lush Baroque, or the mysterious and sensuous *art nouveau*. The shape of the line is another important element of graphological analysis. Similarly as in other cases, the shape itself also describes symbolically the features of character. Obviously, we analyse lines of handwriting mainly from the point of view of symbolic space.

At this point we will use a diagram again to show the convergence of shape of lines of handwriting in a row and symbolic shape of the mouth corresponding to a frame of mind."

"May I ask for the picture again, I think I know what we're talking about, but it would be good to make sure."

"I'll draw it for you in a moment, Mark." He picked up his notebook and sketched a diagram that he gave me after a moment.

"I think you will already definitely find it easier to understand the symbolic meaning of the layout of the lines.
Figure a—shows depression, b—determination, c—optimism.

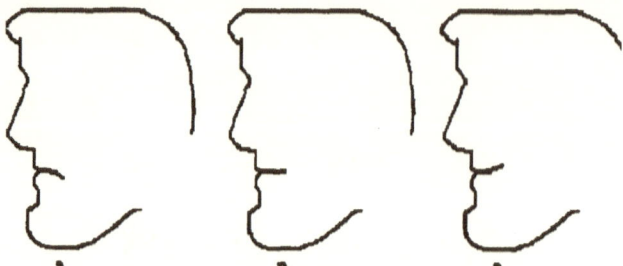

Fig. 36. Symbolic convergence of lines of mouth and handwriting

Rising lines of handwriting:
There are typical features of handwriting of ambitious people, with high aspirations, people of action. Such people usually look at the world optimistically. From the previous diagram in which we compared the lines of handwriting to the line of the mouth, you noticed that rising corners symbolize smiling and serenity.

But, we usually write text on graph paper. Printed lines on the paper guide us and indicate how to steer the line of handwriting—indeed, it's easier to analyse the handwriting without the props, that is on plain paper. However, even on lined or graph paper the features are visible, although to a lesser extent.

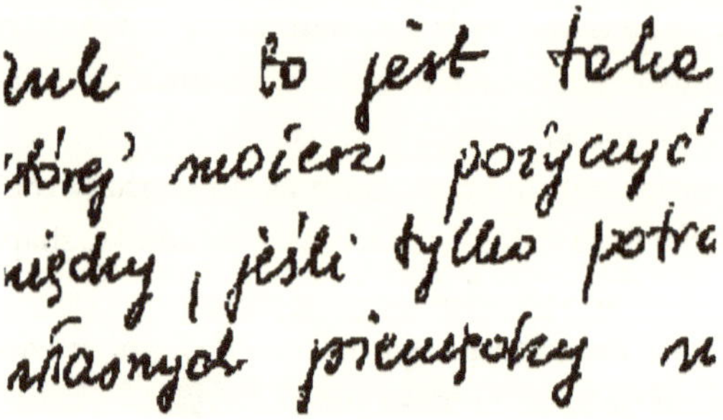

Fig. 37. Rising handwriting

Wavy handwriting line:
This way of writing is reminiscent of waves in water. It tells us of variable moods, susceptibility to influence, and at the same time flexibility and a sense of diplomacy.

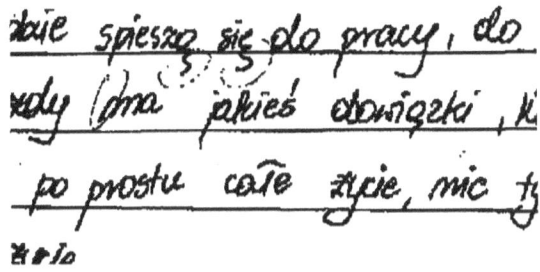

Fig. 38. Wavy handwriting

Straight handwriting:

Especially when the handwriting has no props, that is writing on plain paper, it characterizes an internally strong person, self-confident, highly persistent in action.

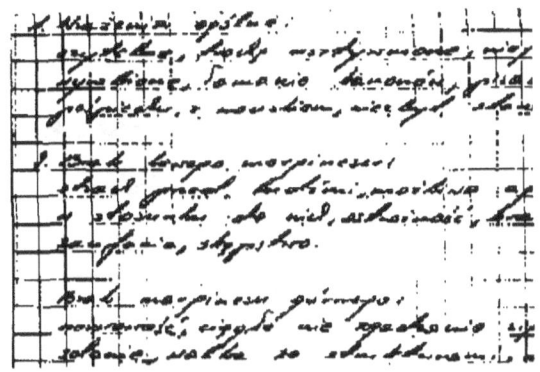

Fig. 39. Straight handwriting

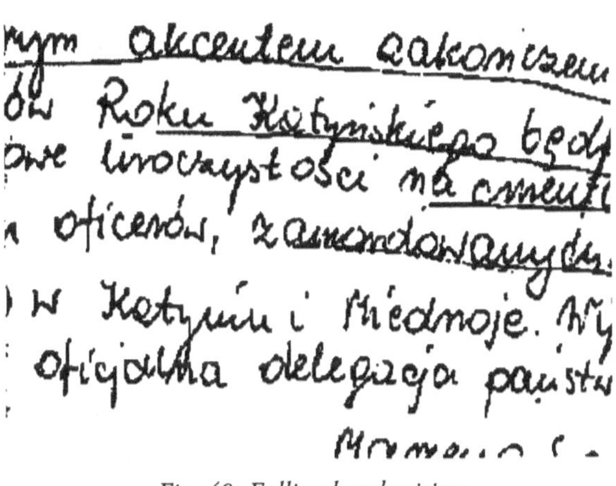

Fig. 40. Falling handwriting

This particular script, which you can see, is on graph paper, but thanks to this you can easily see that the handwriting, how it rises slightly above the level of the line and doesn't lean on it. This is a typical record of people of high ambition, even their handwriting pulls itself upward.

Falling handwriting:
Speaks to us of depression. We mentioned it already, earlier.

Handwriting lines of variable slope:
Graphically present symbolic variation of mood. A writer in this way falls often into depression, one moment enthusiastically in action, until the next change. He is a chaotic and badly organised person in his personal and business life.

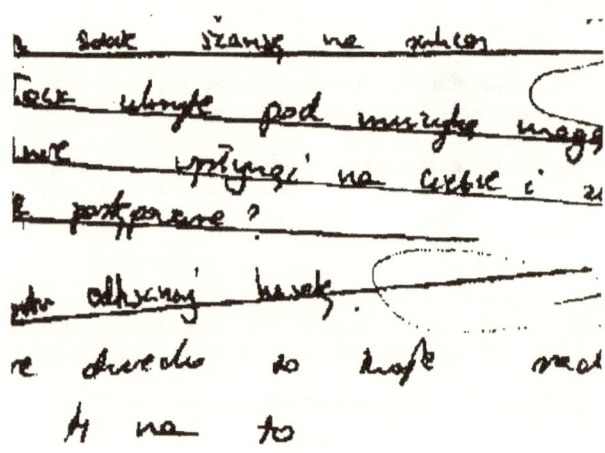

Fig. 41. Handwriting lines of variable slope

Stepped handwriting:
We can interpret this as a particular symbolic description of attitude towards life and life's problems over time. You can easily notice that in the first sample the handwriting is stepped, and in which the words are ascending. If we extrapolate this to symbolic action it means gradual increased involvement in the realisation of any type of task, up to the moment of loss of any interest in it, skipping to another, different problem.

And here is a sample of handwriting where the words are placed differently."—At this point he gave me another script—"In this case it can be clearly seen that the words are descending. They symbolize the feature colloquially known as a 'flash in the pan'. A person with such handwriting is suddenly inflamed with an idea then quickly discouraged when seduced by another passion.

Here you should remember that particular features of handwriting should be confirmed by other graphological elements. That's the only way we can be sure that we're not making a mistake in analysis.

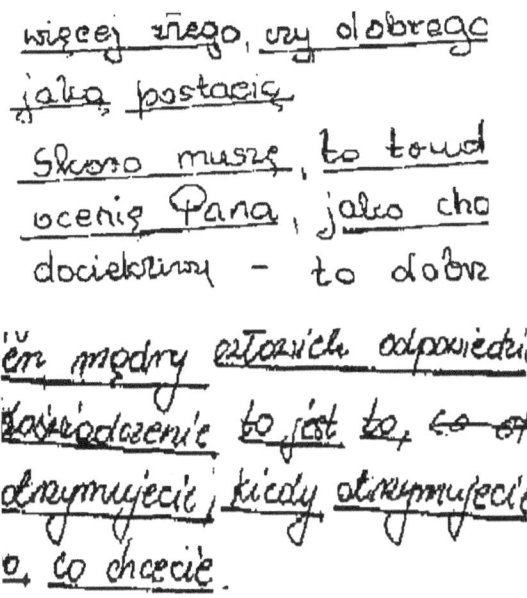

Fig. 42. Two varieties of stepped handwriting

Finally one more essential element in graphological analysis should be mentioned. I have in my mind the paragraph.

The paragraph:
is rather like a graphical indentation in the image of the handwriting on the sheet of paper. Despite their school education people usually forget about the existence of the paragraph as an element of format in handwriting.

It should be used for separating one idea from another in the text. In our analysis it means that if someone uses paragraphs during handwriting, then in life they can also separate essential topics from those less important. They are able to act in an orderly, reasonable and moderate manner. Such a person usually behaves with reserve, and is careful to observe the social norms correctly.

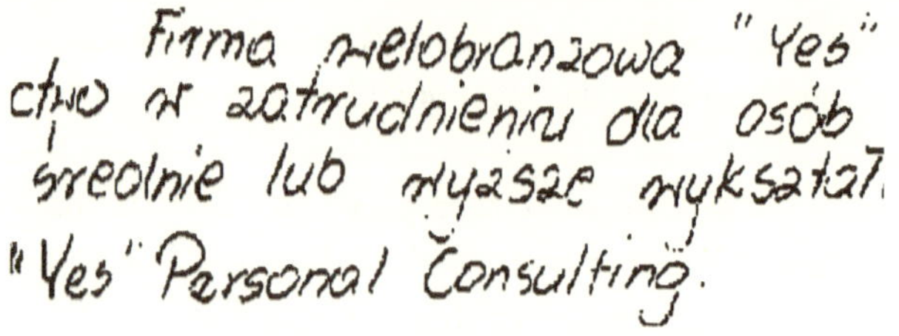

Firma nielobranzowa "Yes"
ctwo w zatrudnieniu dla osób
średnie lub wyższe wyksztal.
"Yes" Personal Consulting.

Fig. 43. A presented paragraph

I think that we should finish our class for today, Mark. During the next meeting I will tell you about the next elements which should be taken under consideration. Now I'd like to say that we should use graphology cautiously and wisely. Once, when Stalin was alive and coming to power, in his own inimitable way, he checked to see who was his enemy. Voting at that time took place in secret, but each voter wrote his 'yes' or 'no' on a piece of paper.

Stalin summoned graphologists and ordered them to find out who voted against his propositions using handwriting analysis. Of course he then treacherously killed his opponents on the council, and afterwards—the graphologists as well."

"That's terrible!"

"Now, graphology is mainly used for the purpose of confirming the authenticity of handwriting, and that—how to do it—I will not teach you."

"Why, Professor?"

"Because you never know how it will be used. Another important direction of application of graphological analysis is personal counselling. When you write the analyses, try not to write too much about the personal problems of the author. You will never know if someone will use it differently and for other purposes."

"But, in that case, is the analysis of writing commissioned by a company, and not the individual concerned, legitimate?"

"Yes. Because after the analysis, an appropriate candidate will be selected for an important position in the company. However, an ambitious but unsuitable candidate for the position in terms of character, will struggle and bring loss to the company. At the same time however, perhaps the candidate could find work for himself much more suited to his personality."

Chapter VIII

LETTER CONNECTION

It became cooler. Earlier there had been a thunderstorm. The Professor closed the window carefully, today he was visibly paler. I didn't know how I should behave. He had heart trouble, and today due to the dramatic jumps in pressure, he could have been feeling very bad. On the other hand, if I were to tell him that he should relax, he would have become angry and felt even worse. I decided to wait and propose postponement of the class, if I noticed that he was having difficulty teaching. He always tried to conceal his weaknesses.

"Mark, we began our study of graphology from the analysis of the most general features. Today I want to tell you about a few basic handwriting systems, into which graphologists divide the script.

Arcaded handwriting:
is what handwriting is called in which the main distinguishing feature is arcades of arches. Have you ever tried to crush a fresh egg in your hand?"

"You must be joking, the consequences wouldn't be very pleasant."

"I'm not joking, there is a particular way of squeezing an egg which doesn't allow you to damage it, despite using great strength. If you were to try to crush an egg at its two ends, you would not be able to do it. The egg wouldn't break."

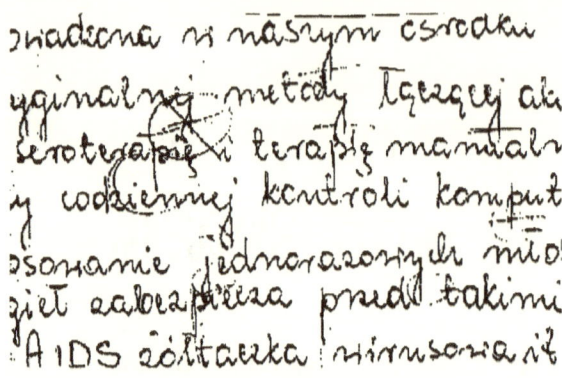

Fig. 44. Arcaded handwriting

"I don't believe it, since eggshell is so fragile."

"Yes, but an egg is like two arches connected at the base. Ancient builders knew about it very well. If they were able to connect two lightly-scaffolded arches, on the basis of these arches they could erect churches, town halls or palaces. Of course, such huge resistance of arcaded arches is only to external pressure.

Fig. 45. Arcaded notation of the word 'mama'

Arcaded handwriting is written by a person who acts formally. They behave kindly and distantly. They appreciate the social forms and conventions. They are very resistant to stress and external pressure. They manage internal problems much less well. They often suffer from nervous problems of the digestive system.

Garlanded handwriting:

is another type of letter connection. Graphically it reminds us of an empty vessel ready to be filled. Long ago heroes were welcomed by garlands of flowers hanging in the streets, to honour them. Those who write in such a way are ready to accept new ideas and suggestions. They are very sensitive to the influence of their external environment. They are friendly and cordial, peaceable and tolerant.

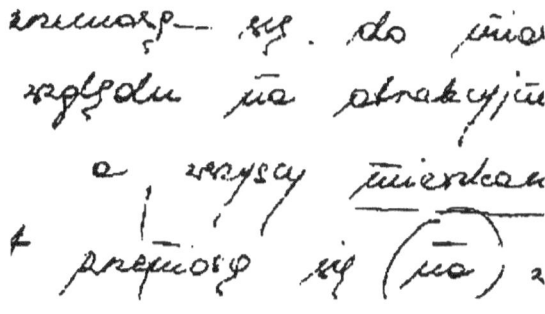

Fig. 46. Garlanded handwriting

Often, however, they are also talkative and very easily manipulated, gullible and soft.

Fig. 47. Garlanded notation of the word 'mama'

Of course the most interesting analyses are those where apparent conflicts are presented, and the characteristics of such a person acquire intriguing details. I will give you some examples.

Arcaded-garlanded handwriting:
If you still recall that analysis is based on interpretation also over time, you shouldn't have problems with understanding such handwriting. It happens that a person starts writing words with typically arcaded letters, and at the end the words are clearly written with garlanded letters. The conclusion is very simple. At the start of getting to know someone we are dealing with distrustful behaviour, distancing and reserve in contact with strangers. However, continuing the relationship we discover that we are dealing with a cordial person, full of warmth, and sensitive. This may be a disadvantage in their professional relations, if we want to have a direct or who is able to maintain an appropriate distance from their employees. In the first stage they are able to do this, but after a certain amount of time, they allow themselves excessive familiarity with subordinates, which may result in a weakening of discipline in the workplace. It's particularly difficult for them to maintain a distance from another person when that person changes from a professional into a personal contact and starts to talk about personal problems.

Garlanded-arcaded handwriting:

is as if the psychological portrait that I presented to you earlier is reversed. It is usually handwriting belonging to people who are sociable and spontaneous in contact with others, but on longer acquaintance it turns out that we don't know them, and the limits of how close we are allowed to get are clearly defined and strictly observed.

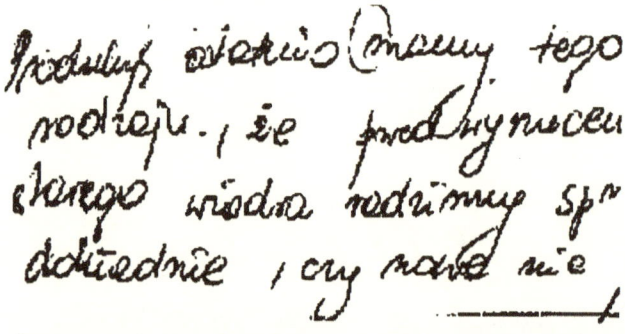

Fig. 48. Garlanded-arcaded handwriting

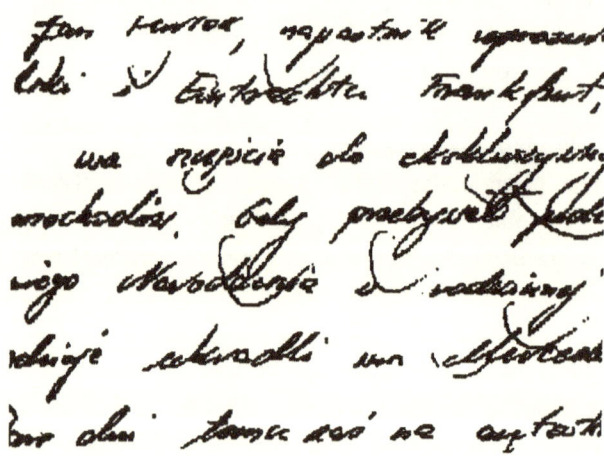

Fig. 49. Handwriting with angular elements

Angular handwriting:

is devoid of smooth letter connections; it has sharp points and is totally lacking in arches. Its appearance reminds us of the teeth of a wood saw. Historically, Otto von Bismark wrote with such handwriting. With him we associate Prussian drill and discipline. Bismark himself was disciplined and sure he was right. Additionally he didn't like objections. Many prominent fascists wrote with angular handwriting. A person writing this way is harsh and demanding, convinced of his own rightness and infallibility.

Fig. 50. Angular notation of the word 'mama'

They possess the ability to command and hate objections. In work they are in never-ending conflicts with colleagues, unless the colleagues toe their line.

As a boss they are very demanding and constantly dissatisfied.

Filiform (thread-like) handwriting:
in contrast to angular handwriting, is built only
from soft connections. Typical filiform handwriting reminds us of a snake crawling.

Fig. 51. Filiform notation of the word 'mama'

Could you tell me, Mark, with what do you associate the symbol of a snake?"

"The snake is the cause of the expulsion of Adam and Eve from Paradise."

"So, therefore?"

"It's the symbol of falsehood, chicanery, disloyalty and slyness."

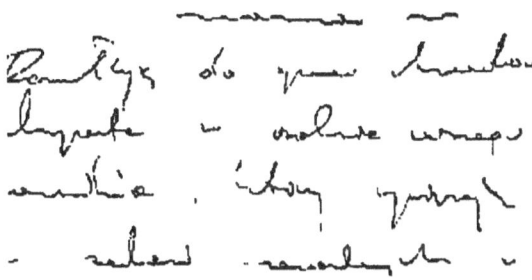

Fig. 52. Filiform handwriting

"Excellent, but we cannot forget about intelligence, diplomatic sense, flexibility, great ingenuity in solving problems. A person with filiform handwriting is not loyal, doesn't like discipline or responsibility.

Once more it is clearly seen how the symbolic meaning of handwriting is congruent with the picture of the character traits of the person.

Separated handwriting:

is a characteristic feature of the handwriting of people gifted with intuition. From the earliest years in school teachers show us how to write in the particular way that the letters are clear, and connected within the word. However, there are people who are not able to do this, and their natural way of expressing themselves in handwriting is by not connecting the letters in the word. The gap between the letters in the word is like a space which doesn't follow logic. Often, people who don't connect letters act irrationally from the point of view of an external observer, but frequently it turns out that they are right, and their plans succeed. They are completely unpredictable to others. They act intuitively and are more inclined to analysis than synthesis of phenomena.

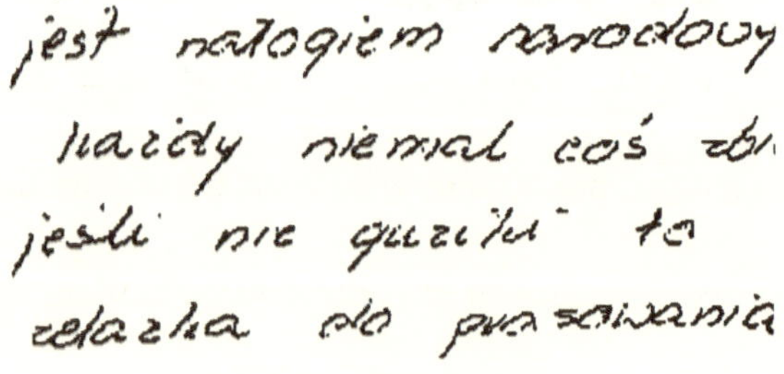

Fig. 53. Separated handwriting

Connected handwriting:

is the connecting of letters within the word. Often it even involves connecting words in a sentence. Connection of letters is the symbolic connection of tasks and actions into a whole. People who write in this way are logical, precise, with greater abilities of synthesis. They are able to realise their goals step by step, and also the instructions of their superiors, but they have a lack of spontaneity and a fresh view of the situation.

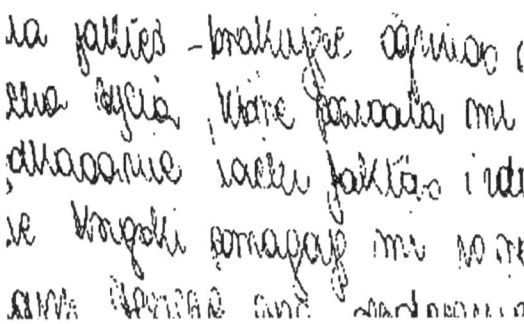

Fig. 54. Connected handwriting

They are more schematic and less innovative. We don't analyse natural gaps arising from the placement of the dot above the 'i' or the 'j' or diacritics in words from other languages. If they are this type of gap in the word, and the rest of the letters are connected, we define this notation as connected handwriting.

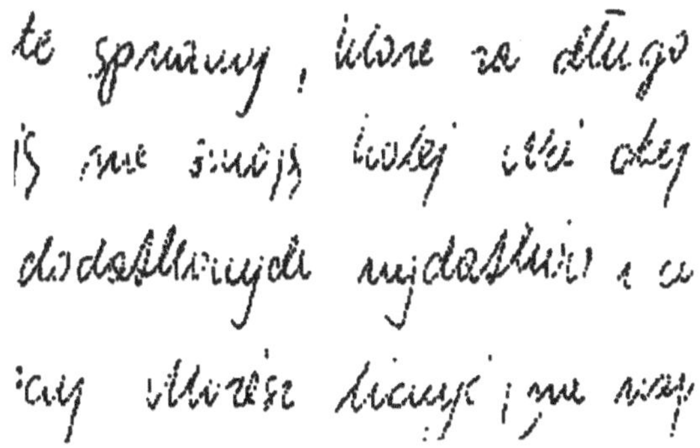

Fig. 55. Handwriting with syllabic connection

Handwriting with syllabic connection:
is notation of the words in such a way that groups of letters are connected, followed by a gap, then again connected in a group. Usually syllables or groups of three or four letters are connected in this way. In graphological analysis we interpret such notation as skilful logical action subordinated to the mind, but also taking intuition into consideration.

Do you have any other questions, Mark?"

"No, I admit that I don't know, today again we touched on so many essential matters that I have to reconsider everything exactly and to practise, so as not to become lost."

"You can do this at home, I would prefer to go to bed."

"Goodnight Professor." I said, rising from the armchair.

"Goodnight Mark, please close the door carefully after you."

Chapter IX

THE SIGNIFICANCE OF THE LETTER

"**W**hat are we going to talk about today, Professor?"

"I think it's time to talk about the symbolic meaning of the letters."

"We talked about that recently."

"Yes, but that which we spoke about was only a part of the greater whole. It is usually so that in the lettering one is given the specific meaning of the letters, based on the method of notation. One is not given the reason why we are able to suspect this, or another feature based on the appearance of the letter. However, in this case we can use a tool in the form of the symbolic interpretation of space.

After the last lesson, we are able to interpret arcaded, garlanded, angular and filiform handwriting. We also know the symbolic meaning of these notations. Now we should become aware of what is meant by **loops**.

Looped Handwriting:

is that manner of writing in which a characteristic loop is often produced before the following letter is written. The handwriting comes back to the left during the writing, before it goes further and writes the next character. The symbolic meaning of the gesture should be interpreted in the same way. Loops are interpreted as a return to the internal, analysis of our own reflections, taking care of our own feelings and experience.

Those who write in this looped manner are considered to be egocentric and having a high opinion of themselves. However, this does not complete the meaning of looped handwriting features.

It occurs that on the basis of analysis in accordance with the triple division of space, we can draw further conclusions. Without even knowing the meaning of the individual letters we can make a general analysis.

Look, in this figure you can see examples of letters which have one feature in common."

"I suppose you mean that all of the letters have loops in the upper part."

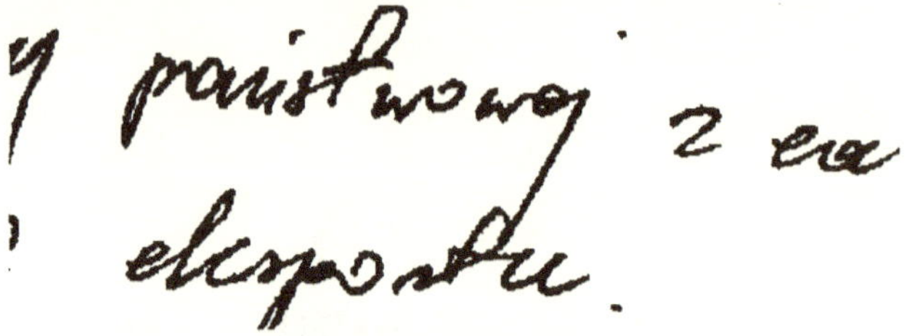

Fig. 56. Handwriting with loops in the upper parts of the letters

"Quite so. If we connect with the earlier symbolic triple division of the space, we can draw very interesting conclusions. Loops mean withdrawing into the internal. The upper parts of the letters stand for dreams and ambitions. Altogether we interpret this way of notation as dreaming, sensitivity, richness of internal experience and feelings.

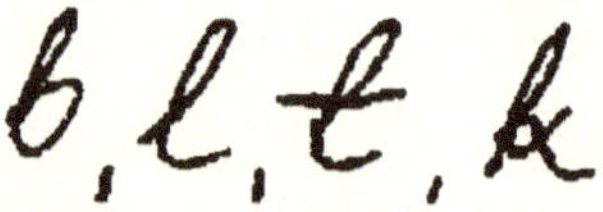

Fig. 57. Loops in the upper parts of the letters

After all, withdrawing to the interior in the sphere of ambition and feelings is nothing more than reflection and concentration of attention in this area.

Loops in the middle parts of the letters:
are interpreted as sensuality, greater sensitivity to terms related to the middle part of the letter according to the triple division of the space. certainly, loops as a symbol of analysis, reconsideration and return, emphasise the area and strengthen the experience in the conscious sphere, that is the part related to action. It is interpreted as egocentrism, even sometimes egoism and having an exaggerated opinion of oneself.

Fig. 58. Loops in the lower parts of the letters

Loops in the lower parts of the letters:

On this level the below-the-line elements which symbolize sexuality and materialism are connected with the looped symbol interpreted as analysis of internal experiences. Generally, loops in the lower parts of the letters are interpreted as a big sensuality and sexuality, and also as the ability to tap into the strength of the subconscious for solving life problems.

You should gradually learn to merge particular features into a greater whole. This is exactly how it is in the work of a graphologist. It's necessary to find the golden mean between a common interpretation for several features of the handwriting. If connection of graphological knowledge with intuition was easy, for sure we could get a machine to do it. For the time being they only help and make work easier, but they are not able to replace a graphologist.

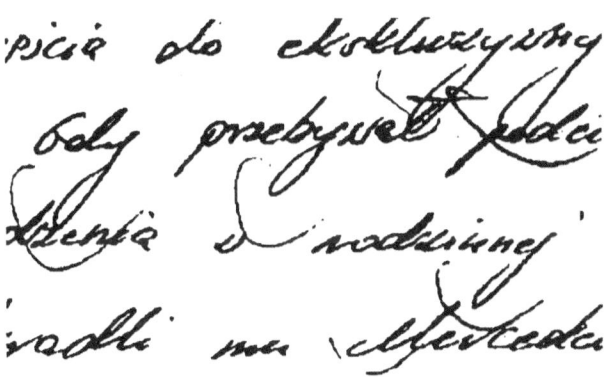

Fig. 59. Handwriting with loops in the lower parts of the letters

Do you remember, Mark, the symbolic interpretative meaning of garlands?"

"Of course, the garland is associated generally with softness, kindness, susceptibility to influence."

"But if there is a looped garland, such as I drew for you, it is interpreted slightly differently.

Looped garland:

is a merging of the features of the garland and the loop. Of course it refers further to kindness, but in a more selfish, learned way. It's the smile given to a client by a saleswoman. She is aware that if she is kind the client will be more willing to make a purchase in her shop.

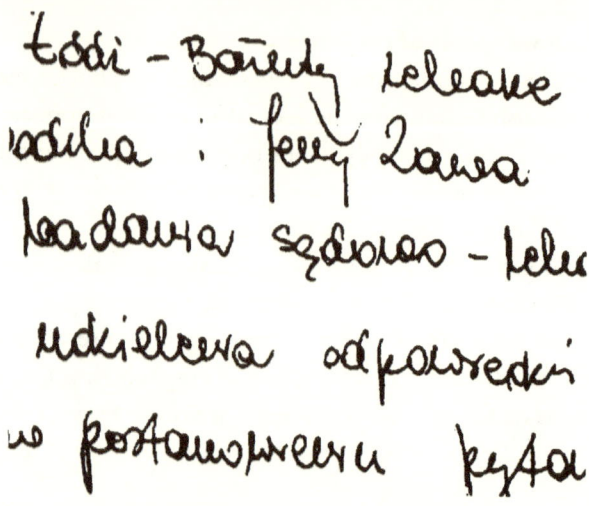

Fig. 60. Handwriting without loops

It is necessary to take into consideration the fact that the degree of exaggeration of this feature in the handwriting is proportionate to the emphasis of the same feature in the character of the individual.

If, for example, the upper loop is disproportionately large, it signifies exaggerated dreaming, even more infantilism.

In the middle part of the letters it is also analysed, if the single-degree letters such as: a, o; or double-degree such as: b, d; are closed or not, and depending on this we can accept or reject the assumption.

Incompletely closed a, o or b, are interpreted as information about exuberance in the speech of the author of the handwriting. It is determined that such letters are typical of talkative people, and those who are unable to keep secrets.

Properly closed letters relate to the abilities of keeping secrets, and discretion.

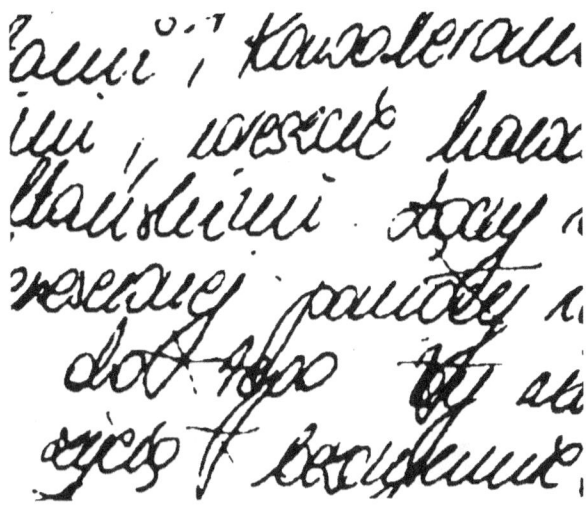

Fig. 61. Looped garlands

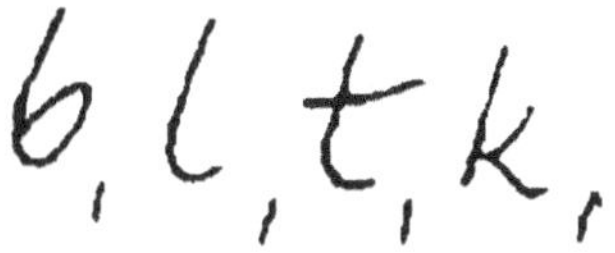

$$b, l, t, k,$$

Fig. 62. Lack of loops in the upper parts of the letters

Lack of upper loops:

we interpret as control of the emotional sphere, and its suppression. It shows that one is led more by the mind that by feelings, sometimes disinclination to dream.

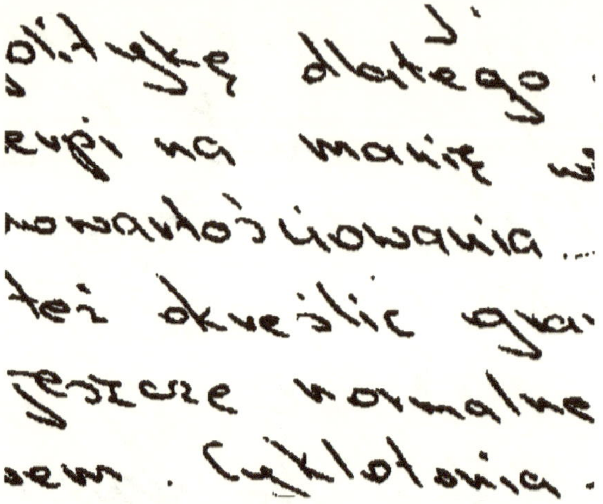

Fig. 63. Lack of upper loops

Lack of lower loops:

this, by contrast, is a lack of ability to fully develop one's sexuality, suppression of instincts, impulses which are inherent in our subconscious.

Fig. 64. Lack of loops in the lower parts of the letters

This should be understood in such a way, that someone who writes below-the-line elements without loops takes care more about their work and career than about their personal life.

We call this 'escaping to work'. Usually such people explain to themselves that they have not enough time for love because their professional activities take far too much time. In effect they fear such feelings, or they were hurt in intimate relationships, which can also cause 'escaping to work' in order to forget. It can also be fear of the repeat of pain.

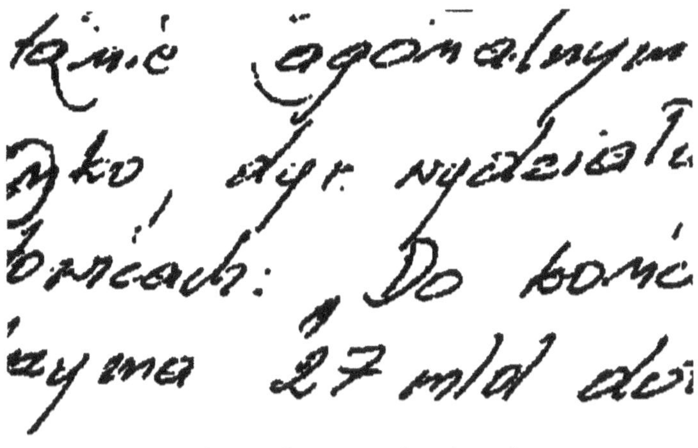

Fig. 65. Handwriting without lower loops

Even if below-the-line elements are decidedly longer than the ribbon, but without a looped curve on the left, we may suspect huge unused potential due to the fact of lack of a stable situation in a permanent relationship, alternatively they find fulfilment in one-night stands, in the absence of a permanent personal relationship.

Remember, however, about the rule that you have confirmation of the interpretation of the handwriting through analysis of other features.

Taking into consideration the fact that graphological symbology changes over time because writing something down requires time, we can weave further speculations.

Lack of upper loops at the beginning of the page:
when upper loops appear in the later part of the text, it means suppression of one's own feelings in an earlier part of one's life; I am thinking here mostly of childhood. It may also be suspected, that a person who writes thus will suppress his emotions more at the beginning of a relationship, but as time passes he will cease such control.

Lack of upper loops at the end of the page:
can speak of difficult experiences in the area of feelings. These caused suppression of natural honesty. Very often the reason for this state is strong external pressures, e.g. difficult economic conditions forcing one to perform difficult and unwanted tasks.

Lack of lower loops at the beginning of the page:
In the instance of this appearing later in the text, it usually indicates a person who didn't have opportunities for sensual development early in life, but who discovered it later.

Lack of upper loops at the end of the page:
shows the natural sensuality of the author, which is pushed into the background due to heartbreak or external factors forcing suppression of this feature.

We may follow a similar train of thought in the situation when loops are replaced by another characteristic element of the handwriting, which is angular writing.

CHAPTER X

THE SIGNIFICANCE OF THE SIGNATURE

It was probably a good thing that we went for a walk. The park was really enriched with shades of red and gold, not only because of intense yellow, and yellowish-red leaves. Even the sunshine in this part of the year is more soaked with red and recalls the colour of old gold.

The professor sat motionless with his thoughts on a green park bench, having behind him a red-green-yellowish background. The whole was illuminated by the sun. Now, he seemed to be an old, sad and lonely man, completely lost and as if from another world.

I thought that I liked him very, very much; that somewhere inside he changed me, not only my way of perceiving the world, but also my way of feeling. The air was cool and wet. The sun had insufficient strength to warm the cooling earth. He shook off his thoughts and asked me:

"Do you feel it? In this part of the year, and in spring, is most clearly perceived the passage of time. However, in autumn even more. In spring, changes are seen, but thoughts turn to summer and not the passage of time.

In autumn, nature bids us 'farewell', and not 'welcome'."

"Is this an allusion, Professor?! Is it goodbye?!" I was fearful of my suspicions.

"Your intuition and sensitivity are very much stronger, Mark."

"?! . . ."

"No, don't interrupt me. We got to know each other, if you remember well, when I had a moment of weakness on the street. My heart has been in a poor condition for a long time. Soon I will leave. I agreed to an operation, and if it is successful, rehabilitation will last for a few months. When everything is over I will write to you and perhaps we will meet in Spring for further graphology study."

I heard clearly what he was saying to me, but simultaneously I felt like a spectator in a strange movie played in a foreign language.

"I don't want you to come to me. You know that I don't have my own children, nor close family, that's how it is. It's the result of the strange, convoluted story of my life. I treat you like a son. I don't want you to see me in hospital. You can take it as a sign of silly, outdated and outmoded male ambition.

If I don't give you a sign in the Spring, it may be that I am travelling. I have always dreamt about it . . . then don't wait. But, we will certainly meet." He stood up from the bench.

"Let's go home. I must teach you a great deal before I leave."

I said nothing, I simply walked beside him, me, an overgrown beanpole of a boy, next to a little, even more than usually tiny, mindfully stepping man.

In my throat something blocked the normal swallowing of saliva. I knew that words were redundant, that he would never return to this subject. He had already made his farewell. Someday very soon, when I knock on his door, no-one will open it.

We settled ourselves into armchairs. Beside us, as usual were weak teas on the old oak table. As usual, without preamble he began to talk.

"A very interesting issue in psychographological analysis is interpretation of signatures.

The signature:
is something exceptional in analysis for a number of reasons; often there is only one source of graphological features for analysis and, since more and more commonly we type letters, applications and other documents on typewriters or computers, and handwriting is reserved for our signature underneath, additionally it is a short record, in a way which can be significantly more consciously controlled.

The signature is a sort of a signboard, in which we present ourselves.

The drawback in analysis of the signature is the limited amount of graphological indicators for interpretation.

The most advantageous situation is when we have at our disposal a sample of handwriting along with a signature. Analysis of handwritten text and a signature more fully captures a psychological portrait of the author of the script.

Due to the wealth of conclusions drawn from it in the course of the analysis, we will mainly concentrate on the correlation between handwritten text and signature.

A general rule in psychographological analysis of writing and signature amounts to the statement that handwriting features reflect the characteristic personal features of the author, whereas the signature reflects additional characteristic features which the author wishes to possess."

"Professor, does that mean that we cannot define even the basic features of a person's character from only the signature?"

"We can, but it is always a decidedly more modest analysis. The significantly more comfortable situation is that in which we deal with handwritten text and signature together. Also, most comfortable is an analysis of a signature more legible than a so-called 'scrawl'. We also look into the difference in sizes of the letters and difference in slope of the handwriting, etc.

A very legible signature:
rather suggests that its owner is an honest person, open, often exaggeratedly overconfident and naïve."

"In that case, how do we interpret an illegible signature?"

"Regarding an illegible signature:
we interpret it as a wish to conceal one's personality and present oneself as a person having something to hide. If our script tells about our personality, and the signature is different in its character from the text, it means that we want to be taken as someone other than we really are.

Legible handwriting with a legible signature:
is usually interpreted as a characteristic of people who are legible to the perceptions of external observers. The person who writes in this way is straightforward, not able to hide their emotions, worries, and it is immediately obvious if they don't like someone.

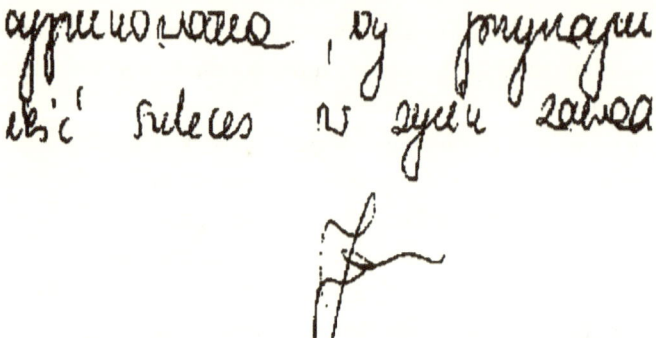

Fig. 66. Larger handwriting, smaller signature

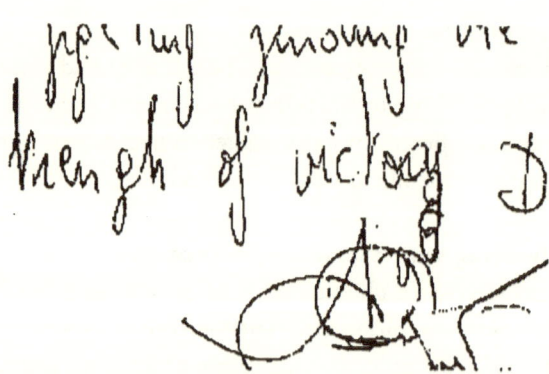

Fig. 67. Legible signature

Legible handwriting, illegible signature:
suggests to us a readable person, often open to the world, who wants to be taken as unreadable, difficult to predict in their behaviour, and more secretive.

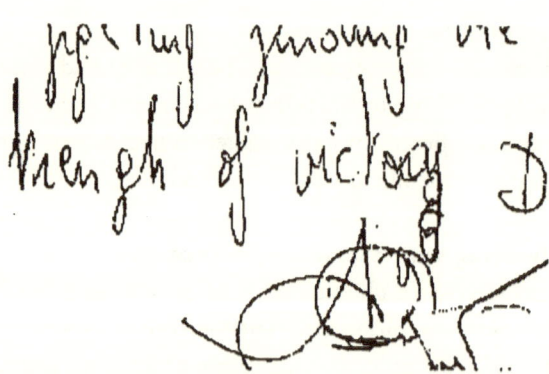

Fig. 68. Legible handwriting and illegible signature

Illegible handwriting, legible signature:
can suggest a wish by the author of the text to underline their honesty. Remembering, however, about the rule that handwritten text is closer to the truth about us, and the signature is only the business card, we can surmise a person inscrutable in their life goals.

Legible handwriting, legible signature:
suggests an inscrutable person wishing to hide their personality from the external world.

However, you must take into consideration the degree of legibility, and I propose that you treat with more rigour the handwriting of greater illegibility."

"Professor, can I in this case, following this outline, try to define by myself the correlation between the handwriting and the signature, in terms of the slope of the letters?"

"Splendid! Try, Mark."

"Handwriting sloping to the right, and straight signature:
suggests that the person writing this way is dynamic, and wants to pass for a balanced and cautious person."

"Excellent, Mark. Discuss some other cases."

"Straight handwriting, and signature sloping to the right:
I would interpret as a characteristic of a cautious and calm person. Especially if the size of the letter is medium or small. The signature in this case will be an attempt to demonstrate their own dynamism and pugnacity."

"We remember, of course, that the degree of slope of the handwriting can vary. The larger the text, the more impulsive we are, especially when the handwriting is big and wide. In the signature however, the more pronounced the slope to the right, the more we want to be taken as pugnacious, decisive in action.

If I have already touched on this subject of the size of the letter, could you analyse, Mark, the difference between the text and the signature related to this feature?"

"Smaller handwriting and large signature:
will surely suggest that the author of the handwriting wants to pass for someone much larger and significant than they are."

"Very nice, Mark, but allow me to develop your idea a little. We measure the size of the signature mainly related to the handwritten text, taking into consideration the size of the ribbon in the handwriting and relative proportions. If the ribbon of the handwritten text is twice as small or less than the signature, we are dealing with a person who wishes very much to emphasize their importance. So great are the grounds for so strongly underlining one's importance in the signature, we should consider it on the basis of a larger sample of handwriting.

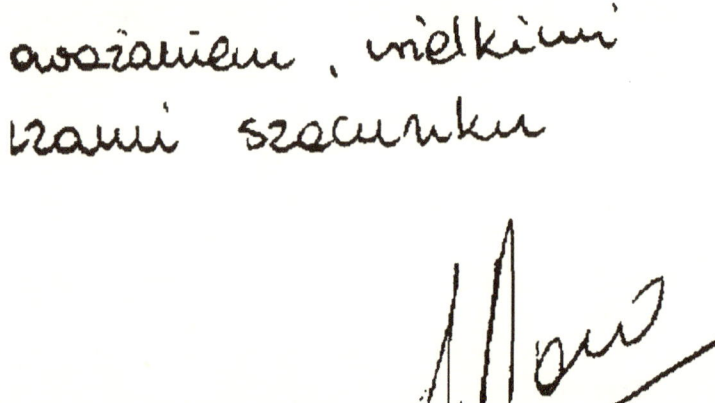

Fig. 69. Smaller handwriting and larger signature

Notice additionally, that **signing with an excessively large signature** breaks generally established norms. They don't want to accept the idea that the signature is supposed to fit in a standard box. They create themselves and don't accept other people not taking them seriously. The signature, however, must be sophisticated. A crude, rather big signature indicates a lack of education or medical disorders of the author.

Underlining the signature:
generally each form of additional underlining of the signature is a wish to show off one's strength. However, we should rather interpret such an evident and obvious sign as a desire. The strength of such a person is rather more dream than fact.

But, try another."

"Handwritten text bigger than the signature:
would rather indicate a person wishing to pass for someone more modest and less significant than they actually are.

It's like a wolf in sheep's clothing. They can be some sort of *eminence grise*, who is interested in genuine power but not necessarily the external attributes of the power."

"Well done, Mark. In order that I may be absolutely convinced that you understand the symbolic meaning between differences in handwriting and signature, perhaps try by yourself to determine some other, any other characteristic handwriting features."

"I will try, Professor, although I feel a little unsure." I admit that I was proud of myself at that moment.

"Garlanded handwriting and arcaded elements in the signature:
should indicate a person susceptible to environmental influences, and wanting to present as cool, formal and following intellect."

"This gives rise to the question, what is the difference between a record such as you mentioned and garlanded handwriting with arcades at the beginning?"

"I admit that I don't know"

"In the case of the signature such a difference is very clear, so it is easier to catch the strong need of just such a presentation without a background in the form of arcaded features in the personality of the author of the handwriting."

"are they the only graphological features connected with the signature?"

"Of course not. When we return our attention to the handwriting and signature and make an analysis in terms of their convergence, we should as the next step analyse the graphological meaning of only the signature.

Until now we have talked about signatures in different degrees of legibility and about comparing handwritten text with the signature.

In the following phase of our research we should concentrate on the word of the signature alone, from the symbolic point of interpretation of intersubjective space.

The symbolic meaning of the signature is identified with the personal seal and word of honour. The signature on the document was and still is a symbolic and legal proof of its acceptance and confirmation of our will. If the signature is so important in our consciousness, then in analysing its form we can reach extraordinarily essential conclusions concerning the personality of the author.

The signature in symbolic expression can have multiple meanings. On the one hand we present our nation and origin, giving our own name. On the other hand it is often also an underlining of the importance of our selves through the exposure of the name, graphically decorated signature or signing with a nickname in the form of a strange diminutive[5], abbreviation of our family name or replacement of the family name with some other alias."

"Does it mean that my forename symbolizes me, and the surname my family?"

"Yes. However, this symbolic reference should be expanded by additional terms.

The forename:

presents the author more individually and privately, is a presentation of the internal, one's individuality in the field touching on one's private and professional life, and corresponds symbolically with one's internal self and home.

The surname:

in turn represents the nation, tradition, professional and representational activity.

Forename and surname written separately:

will suggest in this case ability to separate professional life from private and family matters. A professional soldier signing in this way will be rigorous with subordinates and rough-mannered in contact with others; after returning home from the barracks he puts on his slippers and politely carries out all the orders of his beloved, and doesn't forget to buy her favourite chocolates.

Fig. 70. Forename and surname written separately

---

[5] Polish customs surrounding names and forms of address are complex. Forenames in particular may take many forms, depending on various factors, including the level of formality appropriate to the occasion. For example, a man named Jerzy [pronounced *ye-zhih* where the *zh* is like the s in pleasure] would be called Jurek [*yoorek*] by his friends and close colleagues, but possibly Jureczku [*yoorechkoo*] by his mother or wife.

Forename and surname written together:

suggests that the person signing thus is not able to separate professional matters from their personal. Even at home, they don't make a distinction, and behave the same way as at work. Often a company director is still a director at home, and the politician tries to explain prosaic matters to his wife as though speaking to an election rally.

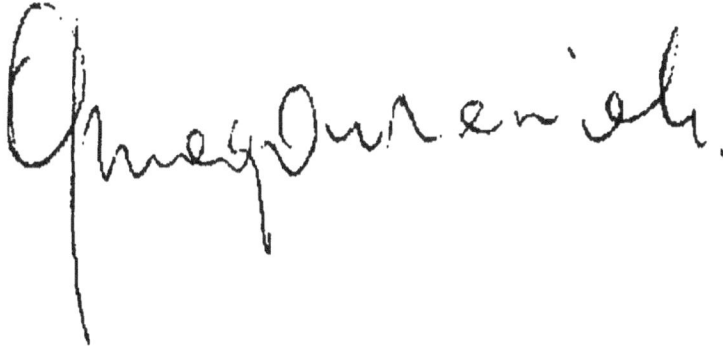

Fig. 71. Forename and surname written together

As you remember the polish school of graphology refers in its tradition to the psychospatial symbolism of Rafal Szerman. He first pointed out that a signature is often a pictorial record of the basic problems and affairs of the author.

For confirmation of his thesis he gives an example of Capelina, who drew his signature in the form of his flying vehicle. A pilot often signs in such a way that his signature resembles a propeller, and a musician often refers in his signature to graphical elements of musical notation. Szerman also gives an example of a suicide signing graphically in the form of a pistol. I can show you right now a signature in which the first letter looks like the sign of the currency of the United States of America. That means that the author would love to be taken for a rich (successful) person, and that money is a very important element in his life. At the same time a cross symbolizing suffering indicates troubles with acquiring money. This line here connecting the beginning of the signature with its end resembles an encephalographic record. On the basis of this it may be suspected that the signature's author is deeply depressed.

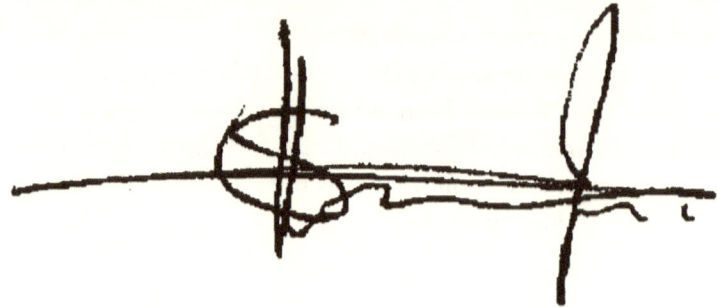

Fig. 72. Signature with first letter resembling American dollar sign

Later it was noticed that in times of peace people who sign with a nickname or pseudonym usually do not accept their father, family or past. People drawing a cross in their signature are often convinced that their main goal in life is suffering. When particular letters or syllables of the signature are sloped at a different angle, alternatively if the signature is clearly broken, we call this 'broken signature'.

Broken signature:
often indicates that the author has a serious family conflict. It may be the parents' divorce or breakdown of their own marriage."

"Is it always like that?"

"No. Such a signature doesn't have to mean a formal breakdown of a marriage. It can be a marriage in name only.

Fig. 73. 'Broken signature', indicating a family breakdown in the home

Women in our culture relatively recently received greater legal autonomy. A tradition which is still extraordinarily strong in Europe, requires that after marriage, the woman takes the husband's surname. we deal with a situation in which women, after a change of marital status from single to married, change their surname and signature."

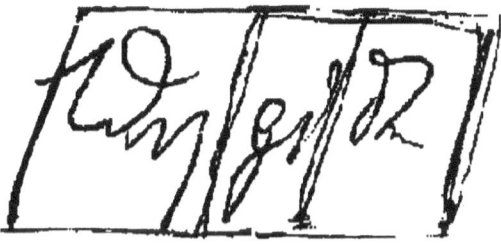

Fig. 74. Another sample of 'broken signature'

"But after all, many women retain their maiden names and use two names together."

"Mark, you should think at this moment and ask yourself the question, whether a maiden name is coincidentally named after the father, that is to say again—after a man. Isn't it, furthermore, the symbolic right to care for and at the same time have authority over 'weaker', 'worse' and—since they don't even have their own family name (from the distaff side)—women. Tracing the history of connection between members of a clan, a family tree is constructed following the paternal lineage. Those connections which are matrilineal—following the female ancestors—are less important. They are only taken into account during analysis of family connections, when the family of the woman entering into the family of the husband, has a higher social position. Even now, it happens that when we are talking about ancestral relationships, we refer to them only in terms of the male gender[6] and there is no female equivalent in the Polish language.

Fig. 75. Signature comprising maiden name and husband's surname

---

[6] In Polish, if Anna (f), Beata (f), Darek (m) and Ewa (f) are all coming to the party in Gosia's (f) car, then "Dareks' are coming to the party".

Obviously, the most important archetypical goal in a woman's life is love, and in a man's, power. If a woman retains her maiden name, it means altogether a lack of full acceptance of total dependence on her partner in questions of finance, law and emotion. Such ladies are usually ambitious and want to make their mark not only in the family, but in society.

Very often such a signature suggests the dominance of the woman in the home, more often following intellect than emotion."

"I admit that I wouldn't have thought that it was possible to look at it that way."

"The signature is quite simply our signboard; we can compare it to coats of arms in olden days, or nowadays business logos. If a woman signs with only her husband's surname, that a feature which we can analyse from a spatial-symbolic point of view."

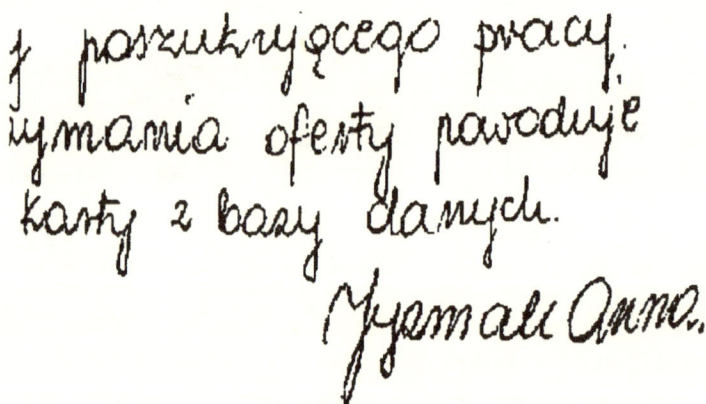

Fig. 76. Handwriting of a woman signing with the surname first

If a woman signs with her surname and forgets about her own forename, it suggests a diminution of her own individual worth in favour of her husband, family, or father if we are dealing with a single woman.

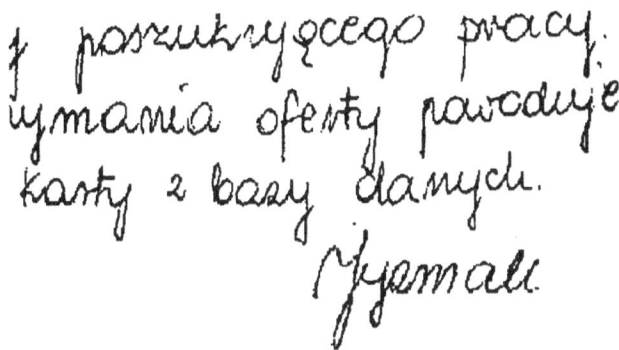

Fig. 77. A woman's handwriting signed only with her surname

It's similar to when the signature begins with the surname and ends with the forename. Clearly, in our tradition we introduce ourselves and sign starting with the forename, then we add the surname."

"Yes, Professor, but on all official forms, it is required to give one's surname first."

"Of course, if we are required by officials giving us the order of filling in boxes in forms, it is necessary to write your details in the specified order. However, family life and social tradition is older than bureaucracy. If you remind yourself of the symbolic significance of the law, offices and structures, it occurs that respect for these types of terms is also no less than the influence of the father and structures at home. Men strongly subjected to the structural influence of the father and needing a strong leader to show them their direction of action, also usually writes his surname in the first place.

Personally, I take the requirement of beginning one's personal details with the surname to be an expression of the dominance of bureaucratic power over humanitarianism and respect for people. It is a symbolic enforcement of the will and a disregard of human individuality as a value, because even in the age of computers, a person who respects others can produce a form in such a way as to be consistent with tradition and not only fit the will and interest of the bureaucratic apparatus.

Taking this sample as an example of handwriting we can, incidentally, suspect some other very interesting features (Fig. 78). Ms Anna not only placed her forename after her surname, but additionally wrote it with a lower-case letter.

The signature, or forename in the signature, written with a lower case letter: is the symbolic additional decreases of her worth. Furthermore the forename in comparison with the handwritten text slopes more to the left. Further interpretative conclusions of such notation tell us about the desire to be externally perceived as a more dynamic person.

A signature written in narrower handwriting in comparison with the text: indicates limits and discipline in the family home. Control of one's actions due to the fear of the judgement of one's parents, husband, father and social structures.

As you can see, we can quite easily interpret the graphological differences between the text and the signature, on condition that one remembers about the intersubjective symbolism of space.

We place the signature, for example, to prove that we agree with the text of the contract, or that we are its author. The signature symbolizes our presence. Animals also sign their territory, thus underlining their right of ownership. For the purposes of this, they use their own olfactory trace, traces on plants or by marking the ground. People can stamp their right of ownership by fencing off their territory and with a nameplate on the door. In marriage, the wedding ring is a symbolic proof of the right to the other person. A uniform symbolizes an army's right of possession of a soldier. It follows from this that a signature as a stamp or seal, the proof of our influence may be presented in various ways."

CHAPTER XI

THE MEANING OF THE DOT ON THE 'i'

That day a butterfly fell through the window into the professor's room. It was an ordinary Cabbage White. We were just about to start the lesson. He asked me to catch the butterfly, put it into a box which he gave me, and release it out of the window, twice warning me not to grab its wings, because they would be damaged. When the butterfly finally settled on the frame of the neighbouring window, I was able to cover it with the box and slide the lid closed. I thought after, why was it so important to give the butterfly its freedom? The professor probably knew what I was thinking about.

"Butterflies are beautiful." he said.

"Oh yes" I stammered.

"Have you ever heard of the 'butterfly effect'?"

"No, I have no idea what that means."

"A very specific domain of knowledge exists on the borders of physics and mathematics, called chaos theory. One of the creators of this trend was Edward Lorenz. He proved that tiny changes in the weather as a consequence could bring about even climate change. He drew attention to that fact that we will never be able to measure all the factors influencing the weather, and that each element, even the least essential, is influential, seemingly significant to the weather, and can result in very significant changes. The motion of the butterflies wings which you released, could have a future influence on whether or not there will be a tornado, in Costa Rica or China."

"No, that's perhaps exaggeration."

"Read about this subject, perhaps you may persuade yourself. Of course this is one of many interesting theses which chaos theory revealed during its development. But already, that which I was talking about indicates that there are no inessential elements. At this moment we can start the proper subject of today's lesson. Today we will be talking about the dot on the 'i' and its meaning."

I admit that I was taken by surprise by the transition from chaos to the dot on the 'i' in graphology. Just as if the professor would like to tell me that all our life has a cosmic dimension and even the dot on the 'i' which we write and which we learn about, has an influence on the fate of the universe. But this is probably an exaggeration . . . Does it generally make any sense? By the way, it could be an interesting book entitled 'The Influence Of The Selection Of Shoe Type On The Fate Of The Universe'.

"The dot on the 'i'" he continued, so that I couldn't expand my own conclusions "we interpret also following the framework of intersubjective psychospace.

It is worthwhile at this moment, for you to remind yourself of the diagram of the triple division of letters. The letter 'i' is a single-degree letter, but it possesses also a dot on the level corresponding to superconsciousness. We can surmise also information concerned with this area. The truth is that the dot, due to the fact that it seems to be an insignificant element for the writer is an extraordinarily precious source of information for graphologists. In the analysis of the dot on the 'i', the pressure with which it is marked, it's size, shape and position are taken into consideration. I know about 60 ways of placing the dot on the 'i' but of course we can analyse this feature even more precisely.

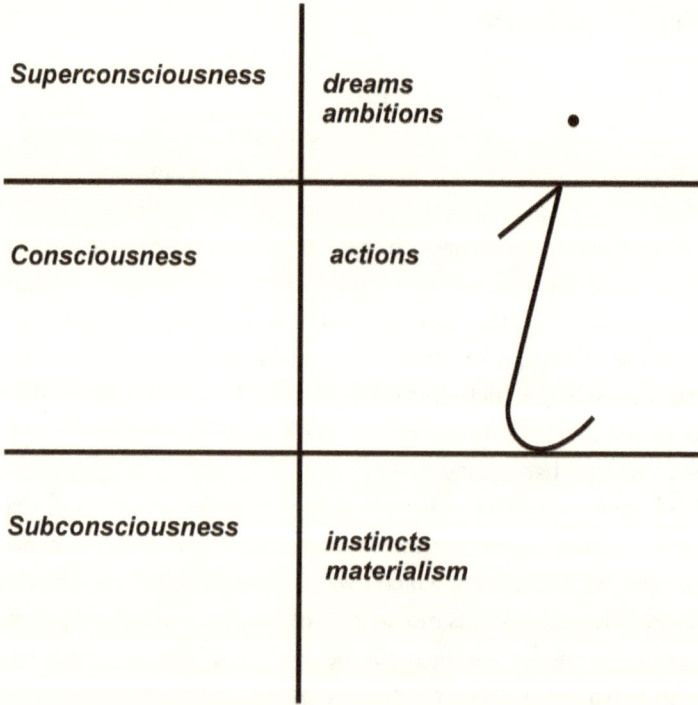

Fig. 78. Triple division of space in the case of the letter 'i'

"But when will I remember all of these methods of interpretation?" On the one hand I was shocked at the richness of the methods of interpreting the dot, on the other hand I was paralysed by thoughts of learning several dozen different interpretations of the one dot in analysis.

"We will not learn by heart all of the features of the dot depending on its appearance. When you catch the elementary rules important to interpretation you will learn by yourself how to build the interpretative meaning, depending on placement in the space and symbolic shape of the dot."

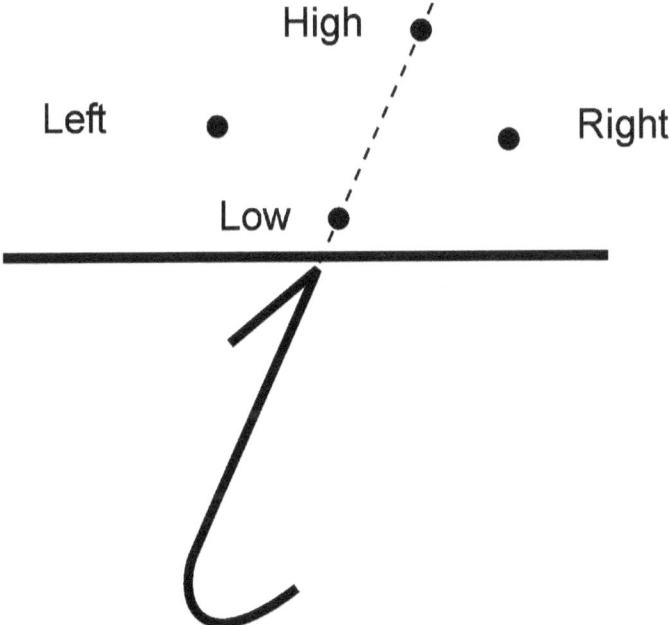

Fig. 79. Correlation of directions in space and the dot on the 'i'

High dot on the 'i':
symbolizes imagination, sensitivity, and if other features confirm it, delicacy. Of course it follows that the dot indicates the symbolic level of interpretation consistent with the symbolism of the space.

Dot on the 'i' shifted to the right:
should symbolically reveal impatience, the desire for fast action and restlessness of the author.

Dot on the 'i' shifted to the left:

is interpreted as a typical way of notation for people often returning to the past, analysing their behaviour, exhibiting cautiousness and indolence in action.

Dot on the 'i' close to the shank:

As you remember, lowness means more mundane, sensual and material. A lower-placed dot indicates that the author is more concrete, vital and endowed with a good memory. With the help of the next diagram, I will explain to you the further symbolic meanings of the dot.

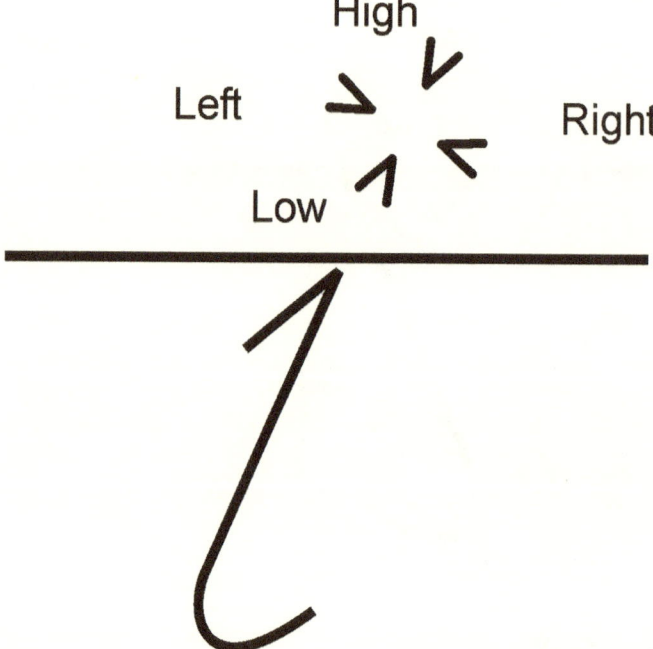

Fig. 80. Basic directions of the dots in arched shapes above the 'i'

The dot on this diagram, or rather four 'dots' are in the shape of an arch. If you look at the script in a magnifying glass, it is very seldom occurs that the dot is really a dot. The arches of the dots, depending on the direction in which they are facing, symbolise greater interest in the respective directions in space. Picture to yourself that the dots in such shapes resemble a dog's muzzle which wants to bite more from the side of the space where its mouth is most open. I will try to illustrate to you one more diagram. You will have to forgive my incompetence in drawing. I hope, however, that this diagram shows the symbolism we are talking about."

I admit that I almost laughed at the awkwardness of the drawing. Nevertheless in the graphical sense he managed to convince me.

"Now I am going to tell you about the individual meaning of the arches.

Fig. 81. Direction of the 'muzzle' symbolically indicates greater susceptibility to stimuli connected with symbolic space

The arch of the dot facing right:
elevated interest in the external world, concentration of attention on observation of people and events (good observer).

The arch of the dot facing left:
augmented interest in the internal world. Observation of one's own feelings and imaginings (egocentrism).

The arch of the dot facing up:
increased concentration of attention on matters connected less with the material sphere and more the idealistic. It can also show that the writer has a good sense of humour due to the arch facing up symbolically recalling a smiling mouth.

The arch of the dot facing down:
suggests increased interest in the concrete, the material. It can also suggest heightened sensuality."

"Are there any other characteristic types of dots?"

"You should get to know still further types of methods of writing the dot."

The dot on the 'i' having a round shape (loop):

"As you remember, a loop is symbolic interest in oneself and the internal. Furthermore, just due to observation (mainly of one's own behaviours) such a person can not make decisions quickly in matters of importance to them. They consider eventualities time and time again, and again . . .

Fig. 82. The dot on the 'i' in the shape of a disc, a bar, plus a stem without a dot

It is mainly interpreted as typical of people having problems with taking decisions, and also having considerable acting abilities. They are egocentric.

The dot on the 'i' in the shape of a vertical bar:

is a symbolic separation of the right side from the left, a sort of cutting between the external and internal worlds. Usually it is interpreted as the ability of critical separation, and that of determining that which is good in the mind of the author, and that which is not.

Lack of a dot on the 'i':

symbolizes negligence, lack of attention to details, and laziness.

The dot on the 'i' connected with a neighbouring letter (bridge):

When someone fluently and originally connects a dot with a neighbouring letter, creating a so-called 'bridge', they should also fluently connect imagination and the creative approach, with practical action and organisational abilities.

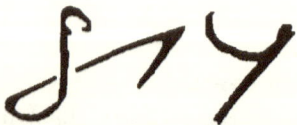

Fig. 83. Bridge connecting the dot with the next letter in the word 'się'

All the elements that we have been discussing should be taken into consideration in the interpretation of a dot adding more graphological elements, about which we were talking earlier e.g. writing pressure. Increased pressure of the dot, shifted closer to the shank from its left side can indicate increased egocentrism, materialism, sensuality and arrogance. Weak pressure in conjunction with other unchanged features of the dot will indicate that the features we discussed earlier are hidden deeper, and in this way the author has insufficient courage to expose them.

Chapter XII

GRAPHOLOGICAL THERAPY?

I mentioned to you earlier about the interesting therapeutic and corrective possibilities, which a good knowledge of psychographology brings. These are powerful influences, about which we usually know nothing, and we are unaware of their strength.

In this case we use the rule that our internal world must manifest itself, the external factors have influence on our interior world."

"I'm sorry, but it seems unlikely to me. This is simply too straightforward."

"I understand that you expect from me examples of such influences in life."

"I would very much like to ask, Professor." I felt embarrassed, since once again I discovered that my trust in his ideas and statements was limited.

"I'm glad, Mark, that you require proof, and therefore you don't just take my words on trust, but you require verification through reason. I refer now to your experience. Have you ever found yourself improperly dressed for an occasion?"

"Yes."

"Did you not feel bad, didn't your consciousness have an important influence on your emotions, that your outfit didn't fit to the occasion?"

"Yes" I could only nod to him.

"And were you ever in a different situation when you were well dressed and saw it in the eyes of others, did you not feel better mentally?"

"Yes, of course."

"So at that time was your perception of reality and outlook on life associated with the way you were dressed?"

"Yes, but . . ."

"That is to say that externalities have an impact on your interior?"

"I suppose so" I admit I felt foolish, I didn't know what to say.

"Would you not feel worse in a dirty, neglected room than in a neat, clean one? Does the environment not affect your mental attitude?

Many people do not realize how serious the consequences are of the subjective perception of space. Yet for this reason, in many fast-food bars and even reputable restaurants, a red colour is used in interior design. It has as its goal acceleration of the blood circulation and stimulation of the client to consume."

"I didn't know about that."

"You remember of course the basic spatial directions, which are the foundations of our world perception.

If we talk to someone while standing on his left side, we symbolically appeal to his emotions and internal sensitivity. Further, being on his right side we impose on him a more thorough and binding subconscious reception of our words."

"Come on, Professor! That seems unlikely." I was shocked.

"For you, the inference is that if you are not well prepared for your classes at University, talk to the professor from his left side; he will accept your explanation more easily.

Returning to handwriting. If we repeatedly determined that it is a symbolic picture of our psychological state and character, then by changing the symbolism of our handwriting we can influence our interior. This is an effect similar to those based on clothing. It follows from my observations, that handwriting used skilfully as a therapy had a stronger impact and for a longer period."

"But you yourself said, Professor, that the character of a man is unchangeable."

"That's right, Mark. That's why, with the help of changes in handwriting we cannot change the character of the man, and especially his temperament. However, we can have a strong enough influence on his behaviour to strengthen some of the individual features and suppress undesirable habits.

Manipulation of the character of the handwriting is very dangerous without proper and rich knowledge concerning the impact of those changes and about the strength of those effects. If you possess graphological knowledge to the degree which I consider sufficiently deep and mature, I will happily share with you the knowledge how in an intelligent and useful way to change some handwriting features."

"DEAR PROFESSOR"

I remember that day when for the first time I had to show off my own graphological analysis in front of you. It had already been a long time since I couldn't wait for our next meeting. I had been knocking on your door for a long time before it came to me that there was nobody there.

I suspected that you had already left . . .

I want very much for the operation to be successful. I believe in it. I decided for myself that I would regularly write letters to you, and share with you my observations. I would like you already to have returned . . .

As always, I attach samples of handwriting with their graphological interpretations. I earnestly request your objective opinion. Often earlier, when I impatiently tried to make analyses and brought them to you, you didn't reprove me for my haste, but always pointed out the handwriting features about which we hadn't spoken, verifying many of my observations. The following lessons proved how much I still have to learn in order not to make mistakes in the graphological analysis of handwriting. When you eventually asked me to make analyses, I have to send them by letter. I hope that in comparison with the previous analyses which I have already presented to you by letter, these are more mature. I have already used the graphological literature which I was able to lay my hands on. I now know that, thanks to your lessons, it is easier for me to understand and learn that which is written in other books about graphology.

Graphological analysis commissioned by my Professor

Maria Kowalska

The author of the handwriting is a sociable person, a little selfish, a little spiteful, she likes compliments and strives to deserve them. In her contacts with people she is like an artful player (gambler)—she can arrange many matters, she knows when, how and to whom to smile, who to chat up, to promise something, in order to achieve her ends. at the same time, she doesn't trust in people, is suspicious and full of prejudices in relation to them. Long ago, she was more emotional and unsure of her own worth, keeping the world at a distance. Now, as if she would like to make up for lost time, she seeks the company of people, but looks at them more critically than before. She bends with the wind, patiently listening to people's complaints and trying to draw them out of their problems. She is vulnerable and soft, thin-skinned, easily touched by a careless remark. She needs support and often feels lonely. She endures thanks to the huge strength drawn from her subconscious, she is guided by intuition. She has an optimistic attitude to life, recently was more impatient and dynamic than usually, more overworked—it can be a reason for her increased irritability, and thoughts about the meaning of life etc. She recognizes authority reluctantly, would like to be important (but she is not one of those who argue about everything, rather yielding to more decisive people than herself). She feels that she doesn't completely fulfil herself, perhaps recently some of her very important life plans broke down, which were connected with her future.

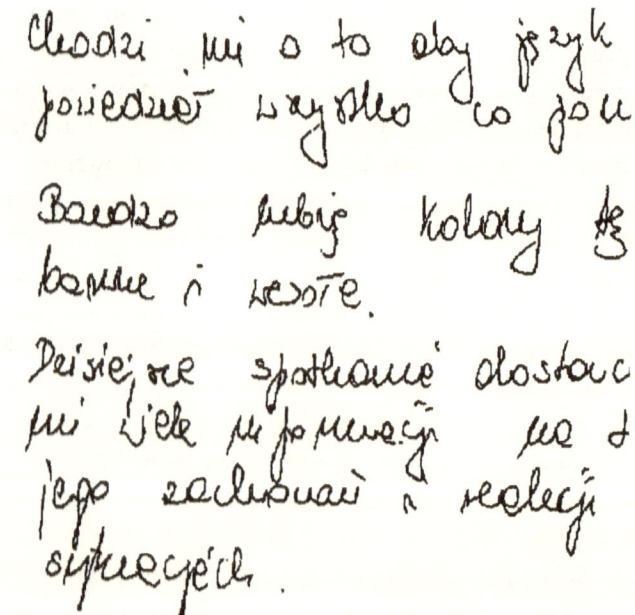

Fig. 84. The handwriting of Maria Kowalska

She dreams about a rest, so as to put into order her ideas, observations about more difficult matters, to be able to make informed estimates about situations which she comes across—it happens that the negatives are interwoven with the positives.

The author of the script is a very intelligent and creative person, unconventional. She is a good observer, has her secrets, which she shares reluctantly although she is changeable, she can concentrate on one chosen thing and has a clearly defined attitude toward it. It happens that, for a good cause, she doesn't always behave according to her beliefs.

She acts in fits and starts, evenly distributing her strength, on the whole, however, moderately dynamic.

However, she thinks quickly and logically, realistically. Gifted with imagination, she tries to bring all her ideas into practice. Recently she has had troubles with making decisions, she debates for a long time and reacts cautiously. She is not one of those very ambitious people, but she would like to be appreciated by the world. Despite materialistic thinking, and wanting possessions, she is focussed rather on working for people and serving others.

She is a spiritually alive person, and sensitive, but she has been impulsive, endowed with huge potential in the sexual sphere. Characterised by her ability to connect normally unrelated thoughts, and spiritual agility. She is hard-working.

Graphological analysis commissioned by my Professor

Paweł Kolankowski

The author of this handwriting is a cultural person, of high intelligence, imaginative and creative. Low self-esteem and lack of belief that persistence will suffice him to take him to the end of his task, caution—will stop him from undertaking many activities in life; it's still possible that similar doubts prevent him from fully grasping opportunities, thanks to which he could have earned more, advanced to a higher position etc.

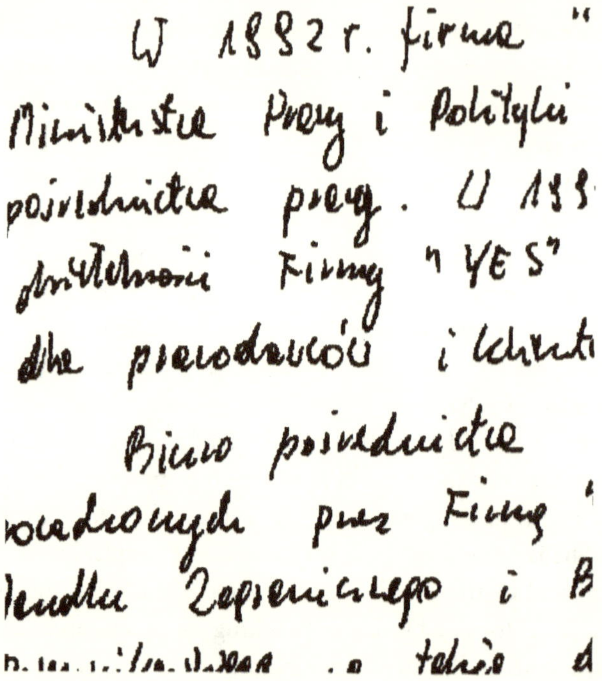

Fig. 85. The handwriting of Paweł Kolankowski

He is the constructive type, a clear-thinking person—he has the predisposition to be able to realise all kinds of projects (which means that he is able to perform all the tasks he is instructed to do, it only depends on whether or not he is brave enough to undertake the task). He is a good organiser, able to separate the very important things from the non-essential. He appreciates the conventions and respects the authorities. In spite of this, he is a person who pursues individuality, therefore he probably prefers unconventional behaviour.

He is one of those multi-talented people, leaning to the scientific. He has the tendency to steer people, to tell them what they have to do (as if he possesses a recipe for the solution to every problem), he can therefore be perceived as a somewhat sharp-tongued person, liking to be involved in other people's business. He seems not to intend to be critical of people, however.

The author of this handwriting is a changeable person—on the outside he can reveal himself to be impulsive, having ebb and flow of energy (performing variable over time, with periods of intense activity and rest). He is a man of substance, able to focus his attention on his chosen goals, and concrete tasks. His speech is precise and accurate. It is important to him to put knowledge in order, making the appropriate comments and taking the correct decisions, allowing him to achieve his aims in the most effective way. He presents himself as a person well-managed in life, forced to choose he prefers a clear situation. He can also be perceived as implacable, not recognizing compromise. He tries honestly to fulfil duties imposed on him; as a superior he can demand reliable fulfilment of his instructions, stubborn. It seems that he likes his own 'moral inflexibility'. If we were able to look into his internal world, it would turn out that he is softer and more conciliatory than he shows, that he is sometimes lazy, has troubles with saving money, and making decisions. It happens that his mood swings from depression, fatalism, feelings of discouragement up to exaltation and euphoria. This causes increased irritability, or perhaps also a tendency to show aggression. He needs support and probably finds it at home in the family. It's difficult to predict his behaviour and decisions are sometimes surprising for people around him. On the one hand he endeavours to tighten his relations with people, but on the other hand he tries to keep a distance, and his behaviour is more formal than social—perhaps he thinks that his position requires this kind of behaviour. He is moderately argumentative, he has quite a big ability in diplomacy, and conducting negotiations. Although he may not show it externally, he is credulous, trusting people and taking everything at face value. Such people are sometimes the victims of schemers and tricksters. All the actions of the author of the handwriting are directed into achieving success—this is probably not a portrait of his ambition, however, he thinks rather that this is the right method for living nowadays.

Graphological analysis commissioned by my Professor

Krzysztof Malinowski
This is a person who likes to draw attention to himself, to be the centre of interest. Although he is a little shy, he wants to stay in the company of many, especially when there is a chance for him to be praised and admired. It may happen that for drawing attention to himself, he will behave a little aggressively or vulgarly, but he doesn't cross the boundaries of tact.

The author of this handwriting is a discrete man, familiar, who appreciates family life. He is ambitious, stubborn and persistent, intelligent and creative. He has a clearly-defined goal in life, and he pursues it consistently and deliberately. He is frugal, so he can gather material goods about which he so cares. He acts reasonably and has a practical and realistic approach to all kinds of problems. He has a good memory, is attentive and precise. Endowed with a strong will, he is able to realise his dreams, although they don't come about easily and quickly. He is a firm and steady person, self-confident and internally self-disciplined. He acts rather dynamically, lately even with some haste, limiting his own freedom, he is cautious and more than ever he is afraid to come up with new initiatives. He is forced into having to save money and a more modest lifestyle. He suppresses his feelings, it may be that he was hurt in this area.

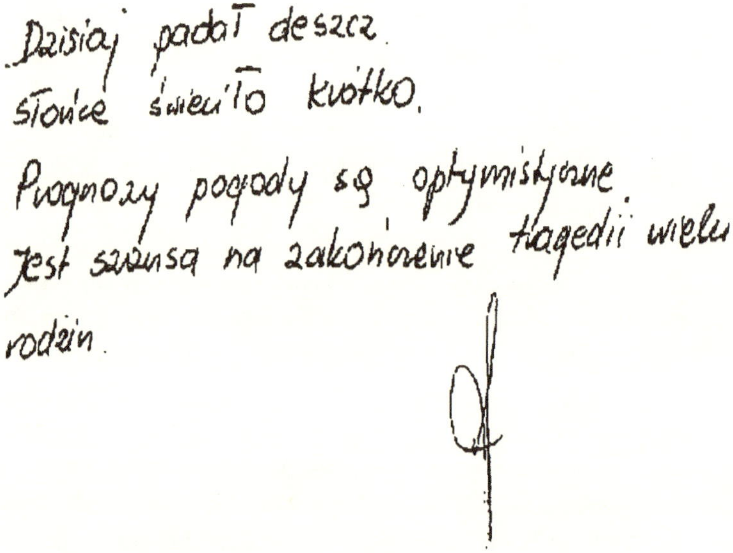

Fig. 86. The handwriting of Krzysztof Malinowski

The author of this handwriting is trying to achieve material success, he probably thinks that money is the ticket to that about which he dreams—to mix with elite company and to have a stable life.

He approaches new tasks unsurely and with reserve, only during their fulfilment, when the final effect and success can be seen does he become more courageous and dynamic. Although for other people he would like to be 'the great' and inscrutable, he nevertheless likes to be appreciated for his achievements, pushing himself to achieve good marks from his colleagues. He possesses organisational abilities, and leadership qualities. He recognizes authority reluctantly, likes clear situations, defends his own ideas and beliefs. It's not easy to convince him to change his mind, since he thinks that he is right. He is unwilling to compromise.

Sociability and the ability to entertain is not his strongest side. If he tries to be like this it is only on the off chance that it will help him to raise his social status. He deprives himself of his personal life in favour of work.

He is a person you can count on but only until the moment when it conflicts with his personal interests. He is not able to be an altruist, and devote himself to good causes, abandoning his own privileges. He thinks more analytically than logically, paying more attention to details, to precision—this can delay the final effect (when it comes to the performance of any task), but increased certainty that it will be exactly as expected. He is impervious to external factors, also to failure. He is capable of starting everything enthusiastically from scratch. It is possible that he is a little greedy.

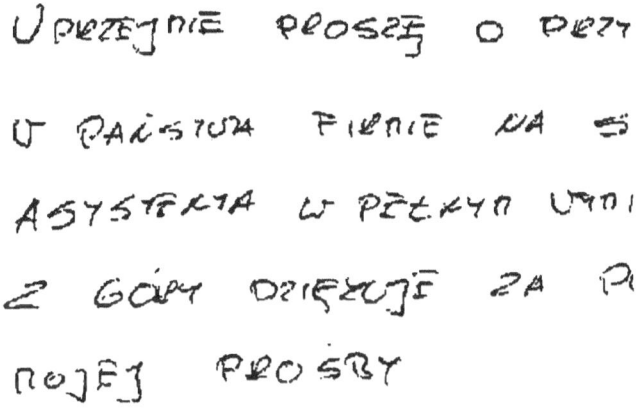

Fig. 87. The handwriting of Adam Kolano

Graphological analysis commissioned by my Professor

Adam Kolano

The author of the script possesses technical abilities. He is unpredictable, hiding his opinions and feelings from those around him, protecting his privacy. Maybe he is not yet a fully mature person. For now he is wandering around his own 'me', directed only toward achieving success, subordinating all his thoughts and actions to the development of his own personality. He is probably able to adjust to the requirements which are imposed by the need to carry out a particular profession, on condition that it will be significant for his future, for self-education and for development of his career. Internally unstable and changeable—to those around him he presents himself as a self-confident person, well-travelled, of great self-discipline. He is very ambitious and would like to be someone unique. He defends his own opinion, so he can become involved in conflicts arising from differences of opinion. He prefers unconventional behaviours. He would like to be important, has a high opinion of himself and at the same time he doesn't trust very much in his persistence, lacking belief in his own abilities. He is afraid that he will not be able to carry out tasks he has begun to the very end. He is a little conservative, has a slightly romantic nature, nevertheless in the present reality he adjusts very well, usually he knows what he expects from life. He is a good organiser, and might be a good boss. He is not yet always able to assess properly the situation, it's easy to 'talk him round', inducing him to fulfil his task not completely properly and logically, by promising him excellent prospects for the future. He lacks intuition in contact with other people, especially when he feels that he is in an advantageous position over them. During discussion he may tactlessly interrupt the flow of the speaker, interjecting his own opinions and comments. There are probably two natures struggling within him:

- ambiverted, tending to cool and strict assessment of situations, concealment of spontaneity, to suppression of instinct and impulses;
- extroverted, pushing him to go out and face the world, seeking new impressions and relationships, directing to the future, tending to hasty, somewhat impatient action. He wants to be free and uninhibited (since he perhaps doesn't feel that way).

This is an intelligent and resourceful person. He can superbly simplify his work, thanks to which he performs it effectively, in less time and without faults in the end product. He is able to connect into a logical whole, things which seem to be impossible to connect. He will be completely devoted to the sort of work that will give him a lot of opportunities for development—probably first of all, however, of personality, and only after that—of his career.

Graphological analysis commissioned by my Professor

Lech Olszewski

This is a man for whom the most important things are feelings. The whole world revolves around them, He often walks with his head in the clouds, in love and distracted. He is sentimental, easily won over by a gesture, by a suitable mood; he is easy to seduce. His dream and ambition is being dominant in emotional relationships. He appreciates woman as colleagues more than men, virtually unable to live without them. In contact with people he is very kind, charming, and even overly polite. He easily adapts himself to new conditions and quickly adjusts to new situations.

The author of the script is an excitable person, vital and active. He is an optimist, who is able to enjoy life. He has high aspirations, willingly exhibits initiative, is full of enthusiasm and even sometimes combative. Simultaneously he is a rather empty person, greedy (despite a tendency toward saving money), sometimes he has been lazy. He would gladly assume the attitude of a child, for whom everything is allowed, and who does not have to take responsibility for himself. He willingly avoids obstacles and problems; if he already faces them, he looks for the fastest way to exit the situation (via the path of least resistance).

He is a skilful diplomat, able to reconcile two conflicting sides. He himself tries not to cause conflicts; it's easy to reach agreement with him—accepting compromise, he tries not to upset anybody. He is productive, he can afford to have remarkable ideas. However, he doesn't always fancy applying his ingenuity. He is also able to think objectively and constructively, and is talented in the sciences. Endowed with a vivid imagination and artistic taste, he is not always well understood by those around him.

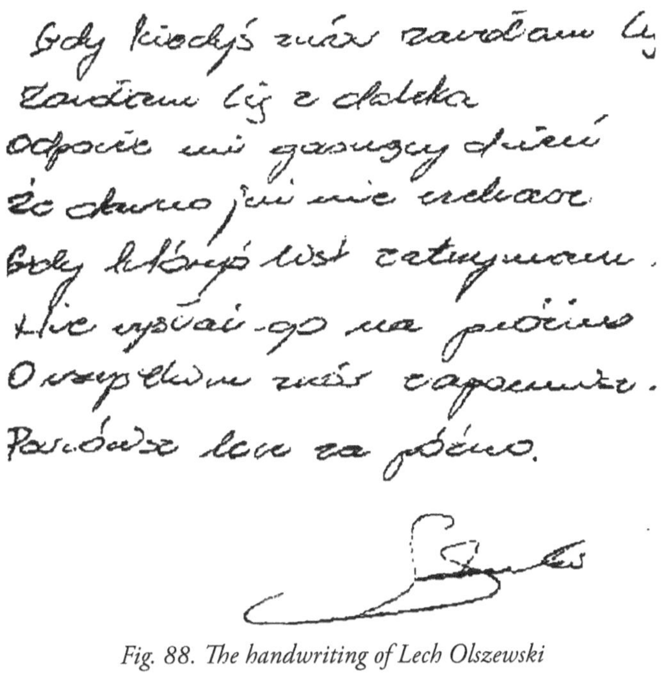

Fig. 88. The handwriting of Lech Olszewski

Afraid of what the future holds, risk-averse, he is suspicious and hesitant, it can happen that he wastes opportunities that fall into his lap.

He is a good observer, likes the company of people, but he feels a little lonely being among them. He then withdraws inside himself, analyses himself, returning in his thoughts to the past. He tries to be discrete, both in professional and personal matters. An exception might be a wish to spin tales about women in his life, love conquests etc. At the same time he is always interested in other people's business, he has even sometimes been nosy. He likes to be noticed by the people around him; with this goes the need to impress (also women—as a man), and he wishes to make a big impact. Money holds no small significance for him, however he tries to camouflage the will to possess it (he certainly thinks that conversations about money are too mundane). That's why it is possible that when he cares to increase his salary, he won't directly approach the boss, he will hedge, make suggestions and maybe someone else will eventually make the request on his behalf.

The author of the script is a person who is able to focus on precisely-defined goals—and aim for them, if they are not too distant and don't demand too much effort and sacrifice. He doesn't like to take the final decision; he reluctantly accepts rules and conventions generally recognized as norms. In front of other people he tries to show himself as much smarter and more mysterious than he is in reality. He doesn't take some actions, he is afraid that he will not be able to finish what he has started.

Graphological analysis commissioned by my Professor

Mariusz Kolasa

The author of this script is a very good observer, he needs close contact with those around him, he also prefers work among and with people. He is a little lazy and a bit of a slob. He feels good in situations where something is always happening, when intuition is more useful than organisational sense. He doesn't like to take on responsibility, whenever possible he tries to avoid liabilities.

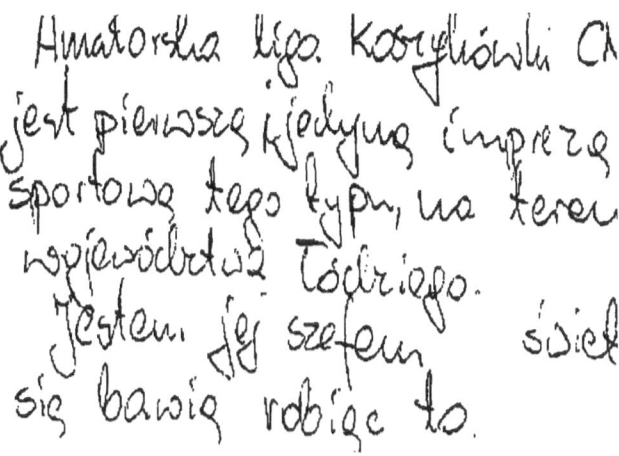

Fig. 89. The handwriting of Mariusz Kolasa

He is a good diplomat, he can sneak between obstacles, emerge unscathed from oppression; he doesn't use force nor tame his disorderly nature—thanks to this he is able to live in accord with himself, harmoniously connecting subconscious, intellect and the simple pleasures which daily life brings. He is not a fussy man, he doesn't endure loneliness well; he is unable to spend a long time working 'tied to the desk', he's not keen on a normal, peaceful life. He must be perpetually in motion, ceaselessly searching for new sensations and lots of company.

This is a man with a high opinion of himself, he happily shows himself to other people exactly as he is in reality. He wants to get the most out of life; he is ambitious, he strives to achieve high social position; at the same time he tries to live in the most luxurious and comfortable way 'here and now'. He likes all complexities and complicated situations; clear and too easy to predict—this is not for him.

The author of this script is a sensual and emotional man (if he doesn't deal well with something, it is with his emotions; it happens that he doesn't know exactly what he wants and what he really feels). He prefers unconventional behaviours, he likes to make a good entrance.

In the presence of all this increased motion we can probably risk saying that internally, in his own way, he is patient and calm. He aims for his goals not as dynamically, but he is able to turn situations as they arise to his advantage. He is not an irritable man (although he is sensitive about his own points), he handles criticism well. He feels very well with himself, and this is the most important. We can suspect him of snobbishness and pride. He desires to live the high life, befriending uncommon people.

He sometimes likes to rebel (however, he accepts the authority of his superiors), he may have trouble with making decisions, especially when instead of intuition or a sense of the moment, he follows prudence and common sense.

He is a mild-mannered man, willing to compromise. He doesn't try to achieve success at other people's expense. He might be a good negotiator.

He undertakes long-term actions reluctantly, the best is when the effects of his work are seen very quickly. He is easily ignited by new ideas; it happens that during the fulfilment of any task his enthusiasm and mood drop; however, he is able to build himself up very quickly, having the next idea on the horizon. He is intelligent and innovative on the practical level, i.e. he can create 'something' having at his disposal defined, real situations and problems. He doesn't like to be materially and emotionally dependent on another person. He can ignore, doesn't pay attention to, certain problems and situations, treating them as insignificant and unworthy of his interest.

Graphological analysis commissioned by my Professor

Alicja Tańska
The author of this script is a person endowed with above-average intelligence; she possesses decorative and artistic abilities; she would also not be a bad educator, psychologist, lawyer or writer. She is sensitive, dreamy; it is possible that she likes poetry.

She willingly escapes from reality into a better and more beautiful imaginary world. She likes to daydream, to dismiss her daily problems. In relationships with people, she maintains distance and is rather official, but at the same time she is socially attractive—she is able to be witty, spreading good humour. She is courteous and altruistic. She clings to tradition, and at the same time she appreciates unusual, sophisticated social forms. She is proud of herself, gladly befriends people who have achieved high social position, are well known and rich. However, we cannot accuse her of being a typical materialist; money is important for her when she needs it to realise a project, and earning it is a consequence of doing what she likes.

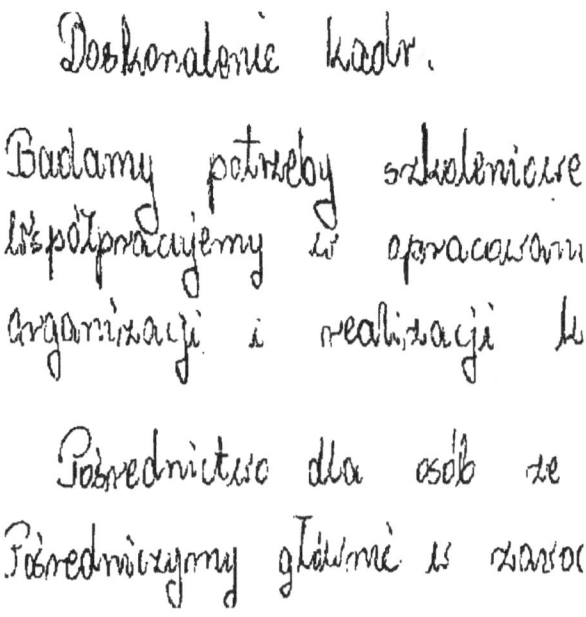

Fig. 90. The handwriting of Alicja Tańska

The author of this script likes to draw attention to herself, to stand out from the crowd, and to be admired. She probably doesn't feel very feminine, she needs ceaseless adoration, compliments and admiration from the men's side.

She may be perceived as a person who follows her intellect, cool and severe, carefully concealing her feelings (although internally she may be seething with passion). She is afraid of being spontaneous and 'hanging loose'. She is well organised and very demanding of herself. It's possible that the high requirements that she imposes on herself and the wish to conform to them (paid for with great effort) cause her to block her own artistic character, not letting her develop it spontaneously, but only under the guidance of her consciousness. She is a person who always imposes discipline on herself; by nature she is hard-working and persistent, but her artistic soul needs more freedom and space than its owner offers it. That's why increased irritability can appear, and feelings of awkwardness and discomfort. The never-changing nature of this situation can lead to continuous dissatisfaction with herself, bitterness, reluctance to make contact with people, can cause the need to criticise others, or even internal aggression.

She goes through life uncertainly, with little courage, being afraid of life's obstacles. Externally she seems to be resistant to knocks, stressful situations; however, she takes them out on herself internally. She is one of those people who needs a lot of time for making decisions, she doesn't make promises lightly, she tries to be responsible for her words and behaviour.

She needs support. She is not the independent type able to manage for herself in life; she likes to have someone next to her on whom she can rely, who gives her advice or even sometimes will relieve her from having to make an important decision. She doesn't know how to take care of herself by herself, and defend her own corner. She is too conciliatory in contacts with people. Sometimes she lets herself be manipulated and used in order to avoid confrontation. She has big plans and she would like to change her life, but over the long haul she lacks persistence and belief in herself.

She has trouble defining her own feelings—in some situations she shows her own true feelings, in others she suppresses them. She blames herself for a lack of realism, practical sense and awkwardness in everyday matters. In life she follows rather her logic, it doesn't often happen that she believes in her intuition. At the same time she prioritises spiritual values over others. This person is endowed with good taste, aesthetic sense and skill in expression.

I hope that I managed not to forget any of the advice you gave me. Also that the analyses were readable and understandable for everyone who ordered them. You emphasized that the analysis emerges from the person, and that the analysis shouldn't be 'flat'[7]. It also shouldn't describe intimate and very personal interests and events. Even now I don't know if my efforts, to try to ensure that the characteristics of these people are rich enough in detail, are satisfactory.

Yesterday I presented my own graphological analyses ordered as samples by a personal counselling firm and I guess the owners were greatly impressed by what I wrote. The main element which prevented them from making an immediate decision is the fact that I am quite young. However, perhaps I'm mistaken about that.

The frost here is biting hard, the thermometer outside the window is showing 15 degrees below zero. I have met a wonderful girl, her name is Kasia. It's New Year's Eve in a few days, so I will take her dancing.

I talk a lot about you to Kasia; maybe it's because I was too small when my father left and I don't remember him. I would very much like to bring Kasia to you one day for tea. I didn't even have the chance to thank you.

---

[7]   lifeless, without character or 'soul'

I will wait . . . I will write more letters, and wait. You didn't give me your address, I still don't understand why, but I will put the letters in a drawer and give them to you, one day.

Your student
Marek

Łódź 11.11.1997

LIST OF ILLUSTRATIONS

Fig. 1. Symbolic picture of the intersubjective division of psychospace

Fig. 2. The correlation between handwriting slope and dynamism in activity

Fig. 3. Inclination of letters to the left

Fig. 4. Perpendicular handwriting

Fig. 5. Variable-slope handwriting:

Fig. 6. Right-sloping handwriting

Fig. 7. Method of measuring the angle of the letters

Fig. 8. The symbology of triple division of letters

Fig. 9. Variable length accents

Fig. 10. Large upper accents

Fig. 11. Large lower accents

Fig. 12. Large central part (ribbon)

Fig. 13. Terms associated with the left and right sides

Fig. 14. Small and large handwriting

Fig. 15. Handwriting with variable-sized letters

Fig. 16. Larger handwriting at the beginning of the page

Fig. 17. Smaller handwriting at the beginning of the page

Fig. 18. The letter 'o' in various widths

Fig. 19. Wide handwriting

Fig. 20. Example of narrow handwriting

Fig. 21. Unduly large letters beginning the page

Fig. 22. Immature handwriting of a 35-year old man

Fig. 23. The mature handwriting of a 25-year-old man

Fig. 24. Front and back handwriting

Fig. 25. Straight left margin

Fig. 26. Wavy left margin

Fig. 27. Narrow and wide left margin

Fig. 28. Widening left margin

Fig. 29. Narrowing left margin

Fig. 30. Wide top margin

Fig. 31. Narrow top margin

Fig. 32. Wide right margin

Fig. 33. Narrow right margin

Fig. 34. Right margin falling

Fig. 35. Symbolic shape of the mouth in depression

Fig. 36. Symbolic convergence of lines of mouth and handwriting

Fig. 37. Rising handwriting

Fig. 38. Wavy handwriting

Fig. 39. Straight handwriting

Fig. 40. Falling handwriting

Fig. 41. Handwriting lines of variable slope

Fig. 42. Two varieties of stepped handwriting

Fig. 43. A presented paragraph

Fig. 44. Arcaded handwriting

Fig. 45. Arcaded notation of the word 'mama'

Fig. 46. Garlanded handwriting

Fig. 47. Garlanded notation of the word 'mama'

Fig. 48. Garlanded-arcaded handwriting

Fig. 49. Handwriting with angular elements

Fig. 50. Angular notation of the word 'mama'

Fig. 51. Filiform notation of the word 'mama'

Fig. 52. Filiform handwriting

Fig. 53. Separated handwriting

Fig. 54. Connected handwriting

Fig. 55. Handwriting with syllabic connection

Fig. 56. Handwriting with loops in the upper parts of the letters

Fig. 57. Loops in the upper parts of the letters

Fig. 58. Loops in the lower parts of the letters

Fig. 59. Handwriting with loops in the lower parts of the letters

Fig. 60. Handwriting without loops

Fig. 61. Looped garlands

Fig. 62. Lack of loops in the upper parts of the letters

Fig. 63. Lack of upper loops

Fig. 64. Lack of loops in the lower parts of the letters

Fig. 65. Handwriting without lower loops

Fig. 66. Larger handwriting, smaller signature

Fig. 67. Legible signature

Fig. 68. Legible handwriting and illegible signature

Fig. 69. Smaller handwriting and larger signature

Fig. 70. Forename and surname written separately

Fig. 71. Forename and surname written together

Fig. 72. Signature with first letter resembling American dollar sign

Fig. 73. 'Broken signature', indicating a family breakdown in the home

Fig. 74. Another sample of 'broken signature'

Fig. 75. Signature comprising maiden name and husband's surname

Fig. 76. Handwriting of a woman signing with the surname first

Fig. 77. A woman's handwriting signed only with her surname

Fig. 78. Triple division of space in the case of the letter 'i'

Fig. 79. Correlation of directions in space and the dot on the 'i'

Fig. 80. Basic directions of the dots in the arched shapes above the 'i'

Fig. 81. Direction of the 'muzzle' symbolically indicates greater susceptibility to stimuli connected with symbolic space

Fig. 82. The dot on the 'i' in the shape of a disc, a bar, plus a stem without a dot

Fig. 83. Bridge connecting the dot with the next letter in the word 'się'

Fig. 84. The handwriting of Maria Kowalska

Fig. 85. The handwriting of Paweł Kolankowski

Fig. 86. The handwriting of Krzysztof Malinowski

Fig. 87. The handwriting of Adam Kolano

Fig. 88. The handwriting of Lech Olszewski

Fig. 89. The handwriting of Mariusz Kolasa

Fig. 90. The handwriting of Alicja Tańska

www.ingramcontent.com/pod-product-compliance
Lightning Source LLC
Chambersburg PA
CBHW020535290526
45786CB00002B/897